Hoodwinked

Also by John Perkins

ON ECONOMICS AND WORLD POLITICS
Confessions of an Economic Hit Man
The Secret History of the American Empire

ON INDIGENOUS CULTURES AND PERSONAL AND GLOBAL TRANSFORMATION
Shapeshifting
The World Is as You Dream It
Psychonavigation
Spirit of the Shuar
The Stress-Free Habit

HOODWINKED

An Economic Hit Man Reveals Why the World Financial
Markets Imploded—and What We Need to Do to Remake Them

JOHN PERKINS

BROADWAY BOOKS / New York

Published in the United States by Broadway Books, an imprint of the
Crown Publishing Group, a division of Random House, Inc., New York.
www.crownpublishing.com

BROADWAY BOOKS and the Broadway Books colophon are trademarks of
Random House, Inc.

*The text of this book was printed using soy-based inks on paper that contains a
percentage of recycled materials.*

Library of Congress Cataloging-in-Publication Data

Perkins, John, 1945–
    Hoodwinked: an economic hit man reveals why the world financial
markets imploded—and what we need to do to remake them/John
Perkins.—1st ed.
        p.   cm.
    ISBN 978-0-307-58992-7
    1. Global Financial Crisis, 2008–2009.   2. Economic history—
21st century.   3. Finance—Government policy.   I. Title.

    HB3722.P465   2009
    330.9'0511—dc22

ISBN 978-0-307-58992-7

Printed in the United States of America

Design by Gretchen Achilles

10   9   8   7   6   5   4   3   2   1

FIRST EDITION

For my grandson Grant Ethan Miller and all his brothers and sisters around the planet; you are the inspiration for us to create a sustainable, just, and peaceful world.

Author's Note

The people and incidents described in this book are real. In a few cases I have changed names and minor details for the sake of anonymity or combined episodes and dialogues to facilitate the flow of the narrative.

Contents

Hoodwinked

Introduction

I was an economic hit man (EHM), part of an elite corps of modern day "hired guns" who promote the interests of big corporations and certain sectors of the U.S. government. I had a fancy title—Chief Economist—and a staff of highly qualified economists, management consultants, and financial analysts who produced impressive reports that appeared legitimate, but my real job was to deceive and plunder the Third World.

Although we EHMs work in many ways, our most common task is to identify countries with resources our corporations covet. Then we seduce, bribe, and extort their leaders into exploiting their own people—accepting loans the countries can never repay, privatizing their national assets, legalizing the destruction of fragile environments, and finally selling those coveted resources to our corporations at bargain prices. When the leaders resist, they are overthrown or assassinated by CIA-sponsored jackals.

We were so successful in the Third World that our bosses directed us to implement similar strategies in the United States and across the rest of the planet. The result is an unsustainable form of capitalism that is the driving force behind the current economic crisis. Despite temporary recoveries, this crisis is the leading edge of a global tsunami.

I jotted down those words while my Icelandair 757 landed very early in the morning at Reykjavik on March 5, 2009, after an exhausting all-night flight from Florida. Staring out into the blackness, I suddenly had the sensation that I was back in the late 1800s arriving by stagecoach in an Old West boomtown, perhaps Tombstone, Arizona, or Deadwood, South Dakota. And that the boomtown's collapse was just another symptom that the tsunami was building energy.

Considered a poor, underdeveloped, and distant cousin to Europe until recently, Iceland's economy had suddenly exploded, rising to the rank of the planet's third wealthiest nation (per capita) on the World Bank's 2007 list. Reykjavik had mushroomed into a boomtown where people amassed fortunes overnight. Celebrities, gamblers, con artists, and economic hit men arrived in droves. Morgan Stanley, Goldman Sachs, and most of the other big Wall Street firms dispatched their necktied armies. Applying a model similar to that used to exploit Indonesia, Nigeria, Colombia, and all the countries whose oil or other precious natural resources propelled them into instant materialism, men and women with my old job convinced individuals and the government to mortgage to the hilt. People embarked on a made-for-Hollywood buying spree. They purchased Miami mansions, Beverly Hills condos, British department stores, Danish airlines, Bentleys and Rolls-Royces, Norwegian power plants, and even an English soccer team. In 2007 the country's citizens possessed approximately fifty times more foreign assets than they had in 2002. Iceland's stock market skyrocketed by a multiple of nine from 2003 to 2007 (while the U.S. market merely doubled). Reykjavik's real estate prices tripled. The average family's wealth grew by three times over a period of three years.[1]

The raw material for Iceland's boom—its gold—was hydroelectric and geothermal power. The glaciers, rivers, volcanoes, and underground hot springs appeared to offer limitless amounts of energy. Because this resource cannot be boxed or barreled, it had to be exploited on site. The biggest of the big energy users, the aluminum companies, came to Iceland in the late 1960s. During the next four decades, as global aluminum demand soared, they convinced Iceland's leaders to construct power plants for the sole purpose of energizing foreign-owned smelters. Alcoa made an offer that would place Iceland on the map—a deal to build a mammoth "water-to-aluminum" complex in the remote north. All Iceland had to do was commit to a very large loan—collateralized by the revenues anticipated from the sale of kilowatt-hours—and hire foreign corporations to build a dam and power plant to generate over 600 megawatts to fire just this one smelter (compared to the 300 megawatts used by all the people of Iceland).

Of course, it was not quite that simple. Scientists discovered that the dam site straddled an earthquake fault line and that the area to be flooded—about the size of Manhattan (in a country slightly smaller than Kentucky)—contained rare ecosystems. The people looked the other way while their government waived environmental laws and issued "special condition" construction permits. In June 2007, Alcoa inaugurated its aluminum factory, built by the United States' Bechtel Corporation. The new factory was slated to produce 346,000 metric tons of aluminum per year, which was ten times the capacity of the country's first plant.

The people celebrated—that is, until they learned that their utility company was hemorrhaging tens of thousands of dollars every hour that Alcoa ran its equipment.

■   ■   ■

On October 6, 2008, the unheard of happened. Iceland's banks, which had grown to many times the size of the country's national economy, collapsed. Losses totaled $100 billion and were rising.

The country's debt had swollen to 850 percent of its gross domestic product (GDP). Iceland went belly up.[2]

As my plane taxied along the runway, I wondered whether Reykjavik would look like Tombstone and Deadwood after the gold panned out, and whether within the hour I would be walking the streets of a ghost town, vacant except for thieves, panhandlers, washed-up gunfighters, and perhaps an EHM-turned drunkard or two.

I had no doubt that Iceland was a harbinger. One of the reasons I had taken this trip was because I wanted to understand the details surrounding the first "hit" of a developed country. If the rest of us did not learn from this nation's tragedy, we were likely to suffer similar consequences.

Iceland, along with the United States and much of the world, had suffered from a specific type of capitalism, a deviant that my business school professors had foreseen and railed against in the late 1960s. The proponents had instilled in business and government leaders from Wall Street to Shanghai a set of values that was leading us all to meltdowns like those experienced by the Third World since the beginning of the 1970s—the time when I joined the EHM ranks—and now by Iceland. The guiding philosophy for this particular form of capitalism is an uncompromising belief in the privatization of resources, the granting of unfettered powers to corporate executives, and the encouragement of debt so extreme that it results in contemporary modes of enslavement—for countries and individuals alike. Based on the assumption that the CEOs running our most powerful corporations constitute a special class of royalty who, unlike normal people, do not need to be governed by regulations, it totally altered geopolitics. Now we have entered a time not unlike that when city-states were replaced by nations—except that today the nations have been usurped by the giant corporations.

The problem, as my business professors understood, was not

capitalism. The problem was the abuse of capitalism and the fact that so many people were infected by the mutant virus. The plane jerked to a stop and I wondered about our chances for controlling the virus before it multiplied into an epidemic.

I walked off the plane, made my way through customs, and then was met by a young man who introduced himself as my chauffeur and was built like a wrestler. He led me outside. The dim light of a breaking morning was diffused by a cold drizzle that felt like it could turn to snow at any moment. As I hoisted myself up into his SUV, I had the sensation that I was clambering aboard a stagecoach, headed for Deadwood.

"I wish I had bought a smaller car," he said apologetically, apparently interpreting my momentary confusion as an expression of condemnation. "But that was almost a year ago. Who could've guessed?"

Not long after leaving the airport, he pointed through the dark mists at a compound of buildings and explained that it had been a U.S. military base with more than 1,200 military personnel—until the Pentagon pulled out in 2006.

I asked if it was a ghost town now.

"Hardly," he replied. "One of our universities took it over. Students replaced the soldiers." He made a clucking sound with his tongue. "Your government sank a fortune into those facilities before departing."

"Why?"

He peered at me, the sort of look a professor gives a student who ought to know better. "I heard the contractors made out like bandits."

Rain spattered against the windshield, and I stared through it onto a barren landscape. Craggy stones were scattered across the rocky surface as though an angry god had shaken his fist and dropped them randomly.

"Volcanic lava flow," my driver said. Then pointing at a snow field that disappeared into a cloud, he added, "Over there is the mountain that caused all this."

I mentioned reading that NASA had trained Apollo astronauts here before sending them to the moon.

"Yeah. That's true," he agreed. "But eventually the trolls drove them out."

"Trolls?"

"Nordic mythological creatures, a sort of combination of elves and giants. Tough little critters." He paused and then gave me a Cheshire Cat grin. "Alcoa hired an exorcist to certify that no trolls would be displaced before building their new smelter. Rumor has it the expert was a charlatan and Iceland's economic problems are the trolls' retaliation." He nodded toward the side window. "See those?"

Through the glass I spotted several tall cairns constructed from volcanic rocks. "The funny statues?"

"Yeah. Sunshine turns trolls to stone. Sometimes they get caught out in the open when the sun breaks through." He chuckled. "Doesn't happen often. We don't get that much sun here."

"Troll economics," I said without thinking.

He gave me a quizzical look.

"Just a thought." I shrugged my shoulders. "What can I say, I'm an economist."

"Oh."

Although I could not interpret his expression, I figured he was wondering what more an economist thought he could take from his country. Those two words, "troll economics," stuck with me. I kept hearing them as we drove on, toward Reykjavik. If trolls had been involved in this classic "hit," they had assumed human form and wormed themselves into jobs with Alcoa, the government, and the banks. An image of a bald-headed man with an impish smile and dragonfly eyeglasses popped into my mind. It was a photo I had recently seen of a trollish Milton Friedman, the Nobel laureate from the Chicago School of Economics. He, more than any other individual, had convinced Iceland, and most every other country, to shun policies that had rescued us from the Great Depression; he had worked his magic to promote that predatory form of capitalism that had brought Iceland down.

"There it is!" my driver exclaimed pointing at buildings just visible through the rain. "The root of all our problems, the first of our aluminum plants, now owned by Rio Tinto Alcan."

I squinted through the windshield wipers. A couple of huge cylindrical towers loomed out of the fog. Stationed above a pier that stretched over the ocean, they reminded me of castle turrets from an old movie about medieval battles. Juxtaposed next to them was a lower building that seemed to stretch forever across the land.

"That one," my driver said, indicating the building that could have housed the world's longest freight train, "is a mile in length. There are three of them. The other two are hidden behind the one you see."

Neither of us spoke as we approached and then drove past the aluminum plant. Not a person was in sight. Nothing moved. The place might have been abandoned, except my driver assured me that it was not. "Operates night and day," he said matter-of-factly.

Like other industrial sites I have visited—coal mines, pulp and paper plants, oil refineries, and nuclear power stations—I found the sheer magnitude overwhelming. It was impossible to place it in any sort of context. Yet I knew that this plant's production capacity, despite increases since its construction, was far less than that of the new Alcoa smelter. I turned in my seat to watch it disappear into the rain behind us.

"There's your ghost town," the driver said, interrupting my concentration. Off to our right were row upon row of quaint suburban-style houses. "All vacant." He shook his head sadly and made that odd clucking sound again. "Great deals, they say, if you're looking for a home in Iceland."

I studied them as we drove on. They did not meet my expectations: no dust-blown streets, tumbleweeds, shuttered dance halls, or doors slamming in the wind.

About forty-five minutes after leaving the airport, we arrived in Reykjavik. "I'm going to take you on a bit of a detour," my driver proclaimed. "The Avenue of Broken Dreams." He turned down a street lined with one magnificent modern office building after another. "Most of them were banks or financial institutions of some sort," he said. "Now, empty."

At first I thought he was joking. It seemed impossible that all these stunning examples of contemporary architecture could be unoccupied. He slowed the car. I pressed my face against the glass and, peering up, saw that many of the windows still had little stickers pasted in their corners. It was uncanny. He slowed even more, and I could see that inside there was nothing. No desks or chairs. Not even curtains. Just huge empty caverns.

"Another ghost town," he said.

"Unbelievable."

"Be thankful you're just visiting." He gave me a look. "I live here."

"I'm afraid we all live here."

. . .

This book is about that "here"—where we are now, how we got to this desperate place, and where to go next.

Wall Street may not look like Reykjavik's Avenue of Broken Dreams, yet. Any more than that avenue resembled the tumbleweed-strewn streets of an abandoned Tombstone. Nevertheless, during the past couple of years, we in the United States have seen the signs. We have been bombarded by images that are shocking and extreme: graphs of soaring unemployment rates and a plummeting Dow Jones; tent cities of homeless men and women outside Sacramento, California, and Portland, Oregon; auto company presidents flying to Washington, D.C., in private jets to beg Congress for massive bailouts; a disgraced AIG announcing that it would pay $450 million in bonuses to the executives that brought it down; former Nasdaq Chairman Bernard Madoff pleading guilty to bilking investors out of billions of dollars . . .

The images go on and on. They depress us. They may have been a surprise to many. But the fact is we should have seen them coming. My professors in the late 1960s did. Many contemporary students did too.

"We had plenty of warnings," Martha, a freshman at Stanford University, told me. "A U.S. budget deficit of over $1 trillion. The mortgage bubble—massive loans doled out to people who couldn't afford them. An extremely expensive war, the outsourcing of jobs, abolishing the banking laws. . . . How could we not know?"

Yet we still deceive ourselves. The occasional periods of "good news" when the stock market appears to revive or gas prices drop lull us into believing that the worst is over. We are Pavlov's dogs; the gong rings and our saliva flows. It is a dangerous illusion that distracts us from dealing with the deeper problems.

"The real story [I wrote in *Confessions of an Economic Hit Man*, published in November 2004] is that we are living a lie. . . . We have created a veneer that hides the fatal cancers beneath the surface."

Unfortunately, a great many people have not wanted to look beyond the veneer. Our political and business leaders have encouraged us to "stay the course." Too often we have fallen back on old platitudes. We have accepted the cancer, the predatory mutant virus of capitalism, as the norm. We have convinced ourselves that we

can continue consuming a disproportionate share of the world's resources and charge it to credit cards without ever paying the usurious interest rates—or the consequences.

"How do you muster the courage [I asked in *Confessions*] to step
out of line and challenge concepts you and your neighbors have
always accepted as gospel, even when you suspect that the system
is ready to self-destruct?"

We have failed to muster that courage. We have allowed our
government to chase the shadows of terrorists across Iraq, paw
through our purses and briefcases in airports searching for explosive
tubes of toothpaste, desecrate our most sacred documents by im-
prisoning people without the right to habeas corpus, and convince
us that criticizing our president was treasonous. We have accepted
the idea that countries whose GDPs were a fraction of AIG's losses
were members of an "Evil Axis" while we have trashed laws that
had protected us from rapacious financiers. We have supported operations that scoured Colombian jungles for terrorists but neglected
to search the ledgers of companies with the power to destroy our
economy.

The election of President Obama was symbolic. Leaping from
conservative Republican to liberal Democrat in one night signaled
a profound change in U.S. voter attitudes. It sent the message that
we want change. The Obama administration's plans to rein in the
credit card industry, impose stricter auto emissions and mileage
standards, create a financial regulatory commission, and implement
other initiatives may shove us back on the path—if they ever pass
Congress. However, the unfortunate and unspoken truth is that the
path will not lead us to real change; it is not a way out of this mo-
rass. It will simply take us on a more circuitous route to disaster. We
must blaze a new path.

My daughter, Jessica, and my son-in-law, Dan, gave me a grandson on September 25, 2007. A couple of months later, on Thanksgiv-

ing Day, I renewed a vow I had made some years earlier to devote the rest of my life to help create a sustainable, just, and peaceful world. My grandson, Grant, had inspired me with a new sense of urgency.

I know what Grant does not—that his life is threatened by the crises generated during my watch. The question is not about prevention. Nor is it about returning to normal—a world where the majority are exploited by a tiny minority. We are challenged today to transform ourselves and our economy.

As an EHM, I participated in many of the events that propelled us into this dangerous territory we know as "normal." As a writer and lecturer, I have spent the past five years touring the United States and other countries, speaking to political and business leaders, students, teachers, laborers, and all manner of people.

I come away feeling hopeful that we are ready for the transformation that will be our salvation, that will save Grant's world.

The first part of this book offers an overview of the root causes of our problems. Through understanding these, we can assess the options before us. Part II is devoted to exploring those options; it outlines a course of action that we can take—both as individuals and as a society—to implement a system that my grandson and all his siblings across the planet will want to inherit.

Many books have been written about the pros and cons of President Obama's economic plan, current schemes for reforming Wall Street, and other short-term policies. These books deal with triage—that is, emergency quick fixes recommended to stop the hemorrhaging.

This book goes beyond the triage. It identifies the virus that infected us and prescribes a long-term cure.

PART I

The Problem

CHAPTER 1

Not a Fluke

THE FACTS

When I was an economic hit man (EHM), I analyzed the statistics of many Third World countries. I never saw any plummet as rapidly as those of my own country, the United States, during the past couple of years. We have all seen the facts in bits and pieces, but some of the more important ones are summarized below, along with my personal observation that things are actually worse than we are being told. (If you feel you are overloaded with facts, skip to the second part of this chapter, "The Challenge.")

The immediate crises began with the U.S. economy. One of the first signs occurred in the housing market where prices peaked to historical highs in 2005 and then began to tumble in 2006. The ensuing declines in other economic sectors further exacerbated the housing crisis. As a result of the huge bets placed on the subprime mortgage market by Bear Stearns, Merrill Lynch, Lehman Brothers, AIG, and the overall financial community, the system imploded. In 2008 Lehman Brothers went bankrupt, and Bear Stearns was rescued at the last minute when JPMorgan Chase bought the company for $2 a share. AIG, Bank of America, and Citigroup would have collapsed as well if not for extreme government intervention in the form of massive bailouts. In the end, major U.S. financial institutions and the markets they dominate lost roughly the equivalent of the total U.S. gross domestic product, about $14 trillion.[1]

A former U.S. senator and a current managing director of the merchant bank Allen & Company, Bill Bradley summed it up at a symposium on April 30, 2009: "The national government has now made about $12.7 trillion in guarantees and commitments to the U.S. financial sector, and we've already spent a little over $4 trillion in this crisis. . . . U.S. taxpayers are into Citicorp for around $400 billion."

Paul Krugman, winner of the 2008 Nobel Prize in Economics, added, "U.S. households have seen their net worth decline abruptly by $13 trillion, and there are similar blows occurring around the world."[2]

The global financial meltdown spread throughout the economy. By December 30, 2008, the S&P/Case-Shiller Home Price Index plunged further than it ever had before. Residential construction dropped by 38 percent. In the first months of 2009, gross domestic product fell at an average annual rate of over 6 percent. Industrial production tumbled 13 percent. The U.S. Bureau of Labor Statistics announced, "In April [2009], job losses were large and widespread across nearly all major private-sector industries. Overall, private-sector employment fell by 611,000," and the number of unemployed people increased to 13.7 million, nearly 9 percent of the labor force. The recession officially entered its sixteenth month in May 2009, placing it on track to become the longest since the Great Depression.

Every time a new statistic was published, it seemed to shatter previous records; the prognosis was increasingly depressing. Corporate inventories fell by $104 billion, the most since the compilation of such statistics began in 1947. Exports collapsed by 30 percent, the largest decline in four decades. Business investment plummeted nearly 40 percent, another record. Home-building activity dove 38 percent. Companies cut total spending at the unheard-of annual rate of 38 percent. Another historic milestone was passed when 12 percent of Americans fell behind on their mortgage payments or went into foreclosure. General Motors, considered a bellwether of economic health, first announced that it would idle thirteen U.S. assembly plants and trim production by 190,000 vehicles; then on June 1, 2009, it filed for Chapter 11 bankruptcy, stating that the restructuring would result in the loss of 21,000 more jobs, the shuttering of at least twelve factories, and the closing of 2,600 car dealerships.[3] Finally, it suffered the ultimate ignominy: It was essentially nationalized by the U.S. government.

The recession infected the entire planet.

The United Nations' *World Economic Situation and Prospects 2009* report projected a global economic decline of 2.6 percent for the year, a huge shift from its prior worst-case forecast for 2009 of 0.5 percent. The report, issued in January, stated, "The global credit crunch has continued straining the real economy worldwide." It forecast that unemployment would hit 50 million over the next two years, a figure that, it said, "could easily double if the situation continues to deteriorate." The United Nations further predicted that world trade volumes would drop 11 percent in 2009, the largest annual decline since the Great Depression.[4]

Yet the forecasts, as dire as they were, painted an unrealistically optimistic picture—the statistics clearly indicated that we were being manipulated and blatantly deceived by our governments and the world's financial institutions. These people were playing the game I had been taught as an EHM: make the future appear rosier than it could possibly be. Do everything to keep people calm. Maintain the status quo. In the statistics I read, the worst-case scenarios were grossly understated. For example, news out of China indicated that at least 26 million people were already unemployed there.[5] If an

additional 13.7 million were jobless in the United States, then world
figures must already have surpassed the United Nations' forecast
of 50 million—by a significant amount. Another confirmation of
this strategy came at the end of the first quarter of 2009 when analysts strove to convince us that the economy was turning around.
However, Federal Reserve forecasts issued in May predicted that
the economy would drop by 2 percent in 2009, a major correction
from the 1.3 percent decline previously estimated. The Fed revised
its earlier unemployment projections of 8.8 percent to 9.6 percent.[6]
It is prudent to assume that these adjusted forecasts were also optimistic and that the actual numbers will be far worse.

George Soros, chairman of Soros Fund Management LLC and
the Open Society Institute and author of *The Crash of 2008 and What
It Means,* shared his advice to President Barack Obama during the
April 3, 2008, symposium referenced above: "He has to reconstruct
the financial system because it cannot be restored to what it was."[7]

THE CHALLENGE

The collapse we are suffering today is neither a fluke nor short-
termed. It is the result of policies and attitudes that began before I
became an EHM nearly four decades ago.

Since World War II, we have been in the process of sculpting history's first truly global empire. Instead of gladiators in camouflage
suits, we sent in artists with briefcases and computer models. They
applied the laser-sharp tools of economics to chisel away at precious
minerals mined from the Third World.

Typically, our corporations identified a country that owned
something they coveted—resources considered vital or strategic
chunks of real estate. Then the EHMs shuttled off to convince the
leaders of that country that what they needed were massive loans

from the World Bank and its sister organizations; however, the money, the leaders were informed, would not be dispensed directly to their country—it would instead pay U.S. corporations to build infrastructure projects, such as power plants, harbors, and industrial parks. "These will benefit you," the leaders were assured, "and your friends"—the few wealthy local families who owned businesses that thrive on electricity, exportation, and manufactured goods. We neglected to point out that the primary beneficiaries would be our own companies, the ones that constructed the projects.

After a few years, the EHMs returned to the country. "Hmmm," they said, rubbing their chins like artists studying a model. "Looks like you're about to default on those massive loans you accepted." When the model began to quake with trepidation, they gave a little smile. "Not to worry. We can fix everything. All you have to do is sell your oil [or some other resource] cheap to our corporations; drop the environmental and labor laws that make it tough on us; agree never to impose tariffs on U.S. goods; accept the trade barriers we want to erect around your products; privatize your utilities, schools, and other public institutions and sell them to our companies; send troops to support ours in places like Iraq . . ."

It is a system that evolved through the subterfuge and economic cunning of people who freely move back and forth between corporations and the U.S. government (collectively, the *corporatocracy*). The leadership is epitomized by men like Robert McNamara, who served as president of Ford Motor Company, secretary of defense under Presidents John F. Kennedy and Lyndon Johnson, and finally as World Bank president; George Shultz, who was a professor of economics and dean of the University of Chicago Graduate School of Business, secretary of labor, director of the Office of Management and Budget, and secretary of the Treasury under President Richard Nixon, secretary of state under President Ronald Reagan, president of the Bechtel Group, advisor to President George W. Bush, and chairman of JPMorgan Chase bank's International Advisory Council; and Richard (Dick) Cheney, who was the White House chief of staff under President Gerald Ford, minority whip in the House of Representatives in 1989, secretary of defense under President George H. W. Bush, chairman and CEO of Halliburton Company, and vice president under President George W. Bush.

Wandering around an art exhibit in Ecuador recently, I came upon a beautifully executed pen-and-ink drawing of an unmistakable Dick Cheney. He had one foot planted firmly on the White House and the other on Halliburton's new Dubai headquarters. He was waving a fistful of contracts in one hand and an AK-47 in the other, and was squatting over Africa and the Middle East, pants around his ankles, to answer the call of nature. Beneath him was the caption, "How the world sees it."

At the highest levels, there is no separation between the people who run our biggest businesses and those in charge of our government. The front lines, however, are manned by EHMs like me; and we always know that the real hit men, the jackals, lurk in the shadows behind us, ready to overthrow or assassinate any leaders who refuse to accept our conditions. On the few occasions when covert efforts fail, as in Iraq and Afghanistan, the military swings into action.

The model was so successful overseas that we imported it into the United States. Many of the same policies and techniques that we EHMs demanded of leaders in the Philippines, Zaire (Congo), and Ecuador were introduced into New York, California, and Michigan. Among the most prevalent here in the United States: the abandonment of laws that force corporations to adhere to strict environmental, social, truth-in-advertising, and other standards that once protected the rights of the general populace; assumption of large amounts of personal, corporate, and governmental debt; privatization of utilities, prisons, and other "public" institutions; increased police surveillance under the guise of "homeland security"; and the use of public lands to serve corporate interests.

I say "successful" but that is true only if you happen to be a member of the corporatocracy, that club of CEO powerbrokers of business and finance who dine with the likes of senators, members of congress, regulators, and presidents. For everybody else, it has been an abject failure. We the people have seen our privileges constantly eroded, from Medicare to public schools, watched the mom-and-pop stores owned by our neighbors fall victim to huge chains, witnessed the usurpation of the media by a handful of giant conglomerates, and we now find ourselves suffering under an economic recession we were told could never again occur.

Although I had been an EHM for nearly seven years, I did not understand the profound implications of the system I was perpetuating until 1978. My job at the time was to convince Panama's chief of government, Omar Torrijos, to assume a huge World Bank loan. Bankrupting his country would assure U.S. control over the canal—despite the recent treaties returning it to Panama—and guarantee that our corporations would be awarded lucrative construction contracts. It was a classic EHM scam to corrupt a leader, make him rich, and place his country in a position where we could exploit it mercilessly.

But Omar was not buying. "I don't need your damn money, Juanito," he said one afternoon. He and I were standing on the deck of a luxurious sailing yacht that was docked at Contadora Island, a safe haven where U.S. politicians and corporate executives enjoyed sex and drugs away from the prying eyes of the international press, and their wives. Omar leaned against the polished mahogany railing and gave me his most charming smile. "I got a fine house, plenty of good food, fast cars, a friend who lends me his yacht . . ."

He straightened and spread his arms to embrace the cockpit where several of his closest male advisers shared rum cocktails with half a dozen bikini-clad young women. "Just about everything a man could want." Then he frowned. "Except one thing." He went on to tell me that his goal was to set his people free from "Yankee shackles," to make sure his country controlled the canal, and to help Latin America liberate itself from the very thing I represented and he referred to as "predatory capitalism."

"You know," he added, "what I'm suggesting will ultimately benefit your children too." He explained that the system I was promoting where a few exploited the many was doomed. "The same as the old Spanish Empire—it will implode." He took a drag off his Cuban cigar and exhaled the smoke slowly, like a man blowing a kiss. "Unless you and I and all our friends fight the predatory capitalists," he warned, "the global economy will go into shock." He glanced across the water at the sandy beach and palm trees of Contadora and then back at me. "*No permitas que te engañen,*" he said ("Don't allow yourself to be hoodwinked").

I am convinced that Omar's attempts to change the system cost him his life. He died when his private plane crashed in June 1981, an incident that much of the international press labeled as a CIA assassination. Although I was stunned when I learned the tragic news, I was not surprised. I had feared for many months that if he did not succumb to EHM efforts to corrupt him, the jackals would get him, just as they had Mohammed Mossadegh of Iran, Jacobo Arbenz of Guatemala, Achmed Sukarno of Indonesia, Patrice Lumumba of the Congo, Salvador Allende of Chile, Jaime Roldós of Ecuador, and so many others before him.

No one in the United States wanted to shoulder Omar's cause. Least of all our presidents. Like the U.S. Congress, they tucked their tails between their legs and sidled up to their masters, the corporate heads who financed campaigns and demanded more influence and power. We the people, the voters and consumers, clamored for cheaper goods, oblivious for the most part of the toll exacted on rain forests, mountain tops, coral reefs, and human workers.

Briefly, in the late 1960s, it appeared that we might shake off our lethargy when a national news anchor, Walter Cronkite, came back from Vietnam to announce that the war was not going as smoothly as our government claimed. His words inspired people to take to the streets, demanding an end to the fighting, and eventually the war became so unpopular that President Nixon was forced to find an exit. But once Saigon fell, we returned to our slumber, failing to explore the underlying causes of the conflict. We ignored the fact that the war transformed millionaires into billionaires and was merely the symptom of a more insidious illness that would come back to haunt us. We watched Cronkite retire, and we stood idly by as his network and all the others were bought up by the corporatocracy, and news reporting was replaced by sensationalized entertainment. We neglected to protest when Clinton's "African Renaissance" supported one brutal dictator after another, as long as the country opened its doors to U.S. corporate plunder and profits. With few exceptions, we did not challenge the logic of sending our military into Iraq after 9/11. We ignored the trade agreements our government struck that were grossly unfair to other countries, the enormous amounts of debt that were mounting around the globe, and the outrageous powers Washington granted to Big Business by deregulating industry after industry.

We celebrated the cult of the CEO, giving the people who manage our corporations unprecedented riches, until the pay of the average CEO grew to more than 400 times the salary of the average worker (far surpassing the ratios at any previous time in history or those in Europe, Japan, and elsewhere). We plastered the covers of the business magazines with the Wall Street warriors who made billions of dollars, in part by skimming profits and creating new and riskier financial tools. It was the old formula of the few benefiting at the expense of the many. We failed to recognize the pathetic fact that in this case, "the many" were us. The recession hit hard, and still we did nothing—except bail out the banks, insurance companies, automobile manufacturers, and the executives who had bulldozed our savings. We did not bother to peer beyond our wallets into the eyes of people who were shooting each other over Nike tennis shoes in our own ghettos or at the ones with skeletal bodies who were starving around the world. We failed to smell the fumes that were suffocating the Chinese cities where our beloved gadgets were manufactured.

The human rights group Amnesty International warned in May 2009 that the worldwide economic decline was leading to greater repression across the globe, concluding that "we are sitting on a powder keg of inequality, injustice and insecurity, and it is about to explode."[8] The Global Humanitarian Forum reported that global warming causes more than 300,000 deaths each year.[9] We ignored all these signs, and countless others.

We watched funding dry up for environmental protection programs; for those nonprofit and nongovernmental organizations (NGOs) dedicated to improving social and living conditions for the poor, the young, the old, and the vulnerable; and for projects dedicated to monitoring and safeguarding the conditions on our planet that make life as we know it possible. We eschewed the changes that would benefit our children and their children. Instead, we complained about rising gasoline prices and taxes, we bought Hummers and iPods, and we supported policies that funded political campaigns and lined the pockets of CEOs.

We deceived ourselves into believing in the efficacy of a system where less than 5 percent of the world's population lives in the

United States but consumes more than 25 percent of the world's resources while nearly half the world's population struggles to survive at or below the poverty level. Where nearly 200 million children serve as child laborers, de facto slaves, working under inhumane conditions. Where poor countries pay $1.30 servicing foreign debt for every $1.00 they receive in foreign aid.[10] And where one continent, Africa, expends four times more on debt payments than on health care.[11]

We read statistics like these, glanced around at each other, shrugged, and tried to convince ourselves that "our system may not be perfect, but it's the best there is."

. . .

We who live in a society that can fly people to the moon, immunize against smallpox, clone sheep, and transmit entire books instantaneously through the Internet continually neglected to ask the questions that would connect the dots:

If 5 percent of the world's population consumes 25 percent of the resources, the transference of this same economic model to China, India, Africa, and Latin America would require . . . what?

If our system is dependent on turning countless millions of children into financial slaves, what does the future hold for our children?

If the industrialized world can feed its appetite for cheap petroleum only by keeping other countries under its thumb and subjecting them to debts they can never repay, our future prosperity and lifestyles will inevitably do what in the future?

We avoided answering these questions because they lead to one inevitable conclusion: Our present system is a failure. We have not wanted to hear that to provide the other 95 percent of the world's population with the same resources we use would require at least another five planets just like ours, except without people. That continuing to abuse the children of other nations will create a world for our children that is torn by ever-increasing violence. That burdening others with debts too huge to be repaid will ultimately destroy our economy as well as theirs.

We have not wanted to hear that returning to "normal" is simply not an option.

CHAPTER 2

Titans Clash

Keynes Versus Friedman

My work as an EHM promoting major infrastructure projects in Third World countries was based on a messianic belief in privatization and profits. This gospel generated the crises that currently confront us—the economic collapse, and a host of other ills: global warming, human rights abuses, the growing gap between the "haves" and "have-nots" of the world, diminishing resources, and rising prices for oil, food and other commodities. What few realize is that the underlying policies are the direct result of a clash of titans. It is a struggle that changed history.

John Maynard Keynes, a British economist who wrote the classic text *The General Theory of Employment, Interest, and Money*, first published in 1936, fought valiantly for the rights of the common man as a key to successful capitalism. And his ideas gained popularity among academics and policymakers before and following World War II. He overturned many prevailing theories about the validity of "free markets," including the idea that unrestricted markets can—assuming that workers agree to reduce their wages—provide full employment. This was a particularly important concept because "free markets" had been used by industrialists to justify union busting and the squalid working conditions that existed in many factories. Keynes argued that large-scale government spending, supported through taxation, instead of sacrifices on labor's part, was the remedy to the mass unemployment that accompanies depressions.

In the 1950s, Republican President Dwight Eisenhower initiated public investment programs, such as a national superhighway network, founded on Keynesian principles. In a successful attempt to avoid being labeled as a "progressive" or a "Roosevelt New Dealer" by his own party, Ike promoted these programs as a necessary defense against the rising "Red menace" of the Soviet Union.

In 1961, John F. Kennedy, the newly elected Democratic president, was guided by a conviction that money from Washington stimulated economic growth. He invested in programs that inspired individuals to expand their horizons and encouraged businesses to innovate. His "New Frontier" promised federal funding for education, medical care for the elderly, government action to combat the recession, and an end to racial discrimination. His Peace Corps (which I joined in 1968) inspired Americans to reach out to people in other countries. His space program—and the commitment to land human beings on the moon—was aimed at funneling public funds into areas that would both benefit and regulate the private sector.

After JFK's assassination in 1963, President Lyndon Johnson took Keynes's ideas to new levels. His "Great Society" launched major spending programs for medical care, education, urban revitalization, and transportation.

Many senior Republicans bought into Keynesian economics as well. When Richard Nixon was elected president in 1968, he increased direct payments from the federal government to individual citizens through Social Security, Medicare, food aid, and public assistance. Such payments rose from about 6 percent of the GNP to nearly 9 percent during his administration. He also imposed wage and price controls on big corporations, and he went so far as to state, "We are all Keynesians."

Yet strong forces of resistance arrayed themselves against Keynes. His ideas were vilified by conservative businesspeople and politicians who resented the limitations and regulations imposed on them by such policies. They complained that unions had grown too powerful and that expensive labor and too many regulations had given other countries unfair advantages.

"Outrageous," Jake Dauber exclaimed between mouthfuls of Indonesian sate during a trip to Asia in the early 1970s. Dauber was president of Chas. T. Main, Inc. (MAIN), the Boston-based consulting company where I worked. He had invited me and several other MAIN executives to join him in the plush restaurant on the top floor of Jakarta's Intercontinental hotel. "Simply outrageous that the Japanese can undermine every U.S. manufacturing business. They steal our ideas and then produce the goods we invented for half the price—all because of our damn unions."

Jake and other chief executives like him searched for political champions. Eventually they were rewarded by an unlikely alliance between a former movie actor turned politician and an economist from the University of Chicago (where George Shultz was dean of the Graduate School of Business) who was soon to become a superstar. Ronald Reagan and the professor whose image had appeared to me in Iceland, Milton Friedman, formed a team that pugnaciously defied Keynes; Friedman's ideas would ultimately be celebrated with a Nobel Prize.

The diminutive academic with the dragonfly eyeglasses at first seemed an unlikely warrior. He had been raised in the enemy camp, as a Keynesian economist. Then, like the trolls escaping the Icelandic sun, he scuttled to the other side. He turned against his former mentor by proposing a radically different policy that he called *monetarism*. Friedman theorized that the government could not manage the economy because people would shift their behavior to thwart it. He believed that CEOs of private companies would serve the public interest better than civil servants. Keynesian principles, he argued, led to "stagflation" (high inflation and low economic growth), the very economic conditions that hamstrung the U.S. economy throughout most of the 1970s. His solution: Further reduce taxes and annul the very regulations that were implemented during the New Deal to bring America out of the Great Depression.

Keynesians contended that Friedman ignored the many imperfections in "free markets." Chief among these was their contention that people do not always behave ethically. Executives may abuse information that is not available to others, such as profiting from information about the introduction of new products and the subsequent changes in stock prices. Financial experts intentionally confuse the public with the smoke and mirrors of obscure language such as "collateralized debt" and "derivatives." Traders who have access to data about goods that are essentially the same but are sold at different prices in different markets—Botswana and Bolivia, for example—use this knowledge to profit from the spreads. Keynesians maintained that without regulations, the market is a petri culture for corruption.

Friedman, however, won the war of the economic titans when Ronald Reagan rode off the silver screen and into the California governor's mansion and then all the way to the White House. Here was a politician who simply loved the mantras "the social responsibility of business is to increase profits" and "less government is good government." Reagan's political victories were the beginning of an era that would be distinguished by the transference of assets from public to private ownership and the dissolution of laws that had protected consumers and investors from unscrupulous business operators. In retrospect, it was an era characterized by greed, an obsession with materialism, excessive debt (corporate, government, and individual), the formation of huge conglomerates, and ultimately the type of corruption symbolized by Enron, Bernard Madoff, and the debacle on Wall Street.

In the nearly three decades following Reagan's election, the multinational corporations prospered while public investment in roads and bridges, water and sewer systems, and hospitals and schools came to a virtual halt. Increasingly, cities, counties, and states were forced to sell sectors of what once had been considered public property to private corporations. It is estimated that today more than $2 trillion is needed to repair infrastructure that was built during and after the New Deal and then neglected as a result of Friedman economics.[1]

The idea that a "free marketplace" would ultimately stimulate the economies of the developing, as well as developed, countries continued to guide many of Washington's policies for years. As president, Bill Clinton, influenced by two Friedman disciples (former Treasury Secretary and former Goldman Sachs CEO Robert Rubin and Federal Reserve Chairman Alan Greenspan), championed "free trade" agreements [like the World Trade Organization's (WTO) agreements, which include the General Agreement on Tariffs and Trade (GATT), and the North American Free Trade Agreement (NAFTA)] that benefited multinational corporations that were major political campaign donors. George W. Bush, elected president in 2000, called upon Friedman to justify his famous "go shopping" advice to the American public after 9/11, his trade deals in Latin America, and even his enormous investments in the Iraq War. He was a staunch disciple of the Chicago professor, as was his father before him, Britain's Margaret Thatcher, Canada's Brian Mulroney, Iceland's Davíd Oddsson, and Chile's Augusto Pinochet.

Ironically, those who railed hardest against government investments in programs that benefit the middle and lower classes incurred huge budget deficits of their own in order to support the military and the corporations that serve it. In the 1980s, President Reagan's Strategic Defense Initiative (SDI) "Star Wars" channeled billions of dollars to military contractors. George W. Bush's post-9/11 campaigns against terrorism here and abroad racked up the largest deficit in U.S. history. He also created countless new billionaires, substantially increased the wealth of the richest Americans while reducing the real income and wages of the rest of the country, and drove the U.S. economy to its knees.

Michael Parenti, political analyst and author of many books including *Democracy for the Few* and *Superpatriotism,* summarized the evolution of the national debt during those years in this way:

> When Ronald Reagan came into office, the national debt was $800 billion. When he left office, it was $2.5 trillion. . . . He also put in the biggest tax program that ever was, but it was a regressive tax. It was a Social Security tax on tens of millions of people. When George Bush, Sr., came in, the national debt went from $2.5 to $5 trillion. Clinton—I'll give him credit for that one thing—he did try to go for solvency. But when you got to George Bush, Jr., for eight years, the debt has gone from $5 trillion to $10 trillion.[2]

When George W. Bush was elected president, the 400 wealthiest people in the United States were worth about $1 trillion. Six years later, in 2007, their worth had grown by 60 percent, to $1.6 trillion. At the same time, the real income of the average worker decreased by more than $2,000.[3]

The consequences of Friedman's free market philosophy came to a head in the last years of the Bush administration, as the financial markets around the globe collapsed, lending to businesses halted, companies laid off workers, and the economy tumbled into freefall. Yet even in the face of such appalling losses, the favored few of the corporatocracy continued to reap huge salaries and bonuses, as if it were their due. These policies resulted in the headlines that buffeted us for the next year, sickening everyone in 2008 and 2009:

- AIG to Pay Out $450 Million in Bonuses[4]

- Countrywide Execs Form New Firm to Profit Off Mortgages, Bank Failures[5]

- Merrill Lynch Paid $10M Bonuses to Top Execs[6]

- Lawmakers Question Bankers on Bailout[7]

- Texas Firm Accused of $8 Billion Fraud[8]

- Contrite Over Misstep, Auto Chiefs Take to Road[9]

- 100 Ex-Government Staffers Working as Bank Lobbyists on Bailouts[10]

- Goldman Sachs Reports $1.6 Billion 1st Quarter Profit[11]

- ExxonMobil CEO Receives 10 Percent Raise[12]

- Survey: More Pay Raises Than Cuts for U.S. CEOs[13]

- Why Are Bankers Still Being Treated As Beltway Royalty?[14]

- AIG Bonuses Higher Than Previously Disclosed[15]

These are the types of headlines and articles one might expect to read in the history books that describe events leading up to the 1929 Crash and Great Depression, rather than on the front pages of twenty-first-century newspapers and websites.

Such headlines are the opposite of humorous; yet, when I read them, I am reminded of a story about Keynes and Friedman standing before Saint Peter at the Gates to Heaven. When asked to account for themselves, Keynes claimed that he had tried to save millions of poor people from starving during the Depression. Friedman stated bluntly that his life had been devoted to ridding humanity of sin.

"How so?" Saint Peter asked Friedman.

"Breaking rules is a sin," the bespectacled professor replied. "I tried to do away with the rules."

■ ■ ■

"There will never be another Great Depression!" It was a refrain heard often while I was a business school student in the late 1960s. My professors were confident that the laws enacted to avoid such catastrophes would protect us. And they were right.

The United States experienced four recessions during the past three decades: one that began in 1980 and lasted nearly two years; one in 1990 that lasted less than a year and was followed by the longest economic expansion on record; one that began in March 2001 and ended in November; and the current one that can be traced to events in 2006 and really got underway in the summer of 2007.

We bounced back from the first three recessions because we were protected by many of the regulations that I had learned about as a business student. Unfortunately, over the past two decades, those laws had been constantly eroded, dropped, or negated. Then, as a nation, we reached a stage where our corporations behaved like spoiled and rebellious adolescents.

Young people grow up believing that they have to do better than their contemporaries—in their studies, sports, art, dance, or with the opposite sex. Excelling for the sake of simply being good at a task takes a backseat to beating out the other guy. One of the stages before adulthood is characterized by a refusal to follow the rules, offered with the excuse that "those things just hamper my ability to compete, to be myself, to really excel."

Capitalism has gone through a similar process. In order for one clothing manufacturer or car company to succeed, it believes it has to lure customers away from its competitors. On a grander scale, this same drive leads to market domination and exploitation. For centuries human beings have clung to a belief that in order to get ahead, communities—including countries—have to exploit their neighbors. This is the foundation for the old military empires—from ancient China and Greece to the British Empire—to today's post–World War II neocolonialism. The insatiable quest to beat out any possible competitors—real or imagined—has been rapidly draining our planet of its most precious resources.

While unrelenting competition is a sign of immature adolescence, cooperation indicates a more seasoned maturity. We associate organizational skills that result in cooperation as symbols of advanced social orders. We are impressed by and avidly study those animals that form cooperative groupings, like wolves, lions, dolphins, and chimpanzees. As human communities too grow more sophisticated, we see advantages in collaboration and therefore form alliances. Thus, city-states became nations, and nations draw up pacts with other nations to support and protect each other, like NATO and the European Union.

One has to wonder why, after World War II and the establishment of the United Nations, the World Bank, and other institutions that were intended to foster global cooperation, the U.S. government and corporate chiefs have continued to promote a model that emphasizes competition and exploitation. Why have the pacts signed by post-1980 Washington, such as free trade agreements, turned out to have been attempts not to unify but rather to divide and conquer the rest of the economic world?

The answer is that in the war of economic titans, Friedman defeated Keynes. The victors implemented a radical system that promoted a world in which millions of people face starvation and environmental degradation and the depletion of natural resources threatens the very survival of life forms as we know them.

Politically, Ronald Reagan's presidential election in 1980 is the threshold year. But the origins of this reckless drive toward self-destruction began nearly thirty years earlier, when Keynesian economics reigned and Friedman was still developing his theories. The first salvo was like that single shot on the Concord bridge that opened the American Revolution. It changed the world. Except this time it was a covert event that occurred on the other side of the planet. It helped convince a young Ronald Reagan to switch from Democrat to Republican, from Keynes to Friedman, from his role as president of the Screen Actors Guild to that of union buster.

I first heard about that event from Claudine Martin, the stunningly attractive, seductive, and manipulative woman who mentored me during my first months as an EHM.

CHAPTER 3

The First Economic Hit Man

My relationship with Claudine generated the darkest inner conflicts I had ever experienced. She seduced me in just about every way a man can be seduced, although I was a willing accomplice. She offered things I craved: liberation from the Puritanical mores of my parents, adventure and romance, mentoring, and physical intimacy beyond my wildest fantasies. At the same time I could sense that I was selling my soul to the world of the economic hit man. I betrayed my wife and most of the principles I had espoused all my life.

It was 1971; I had just been hired by MAIN—a firm of about 2,000 professionals that consulted to governments and corporations. My boss emphasized that the company prided itself on discretion. Our clients expected us, like their attorneys and psychotherapists, to honor a strict code of absolute confidentiality. Talking with the press was simply not tolerated. As a consequence, hardly anyone had ever heard of us, other than those we served. Under different circumstances, meeting Claudine as I did might have aroused my suspicions; but I had already experienced the company's unorthodox methods.

I was seated at a table in the Boston Public Library, just down the street from MAIN's headquarters in the Prudential Center, when I was distracted by a gorgeous brunette wearing a dark green suit.

As she sauntered into the room, strolled along the stacks of books, and sat down on the opposite side of the table, I pretended not to notice.

Knowing that she was studying me both excited and confounded me. I had been raised the son of a teacher in a New Hampshire boys' private boarding school and had never overcome a feeling of awkward incompetence around beautiful women. Although I resisted the temptation to look directly at her, I was terribly aware of her shapely legs. She crossed, uncrossed, and recrossed them several times while I tried to focus ever more intently on the World Bank statistics about Kuwait open before me.

Then she stretched and, without saying a word, rose from her chair. She just stood there for a long moment, gazing down at me.

I studiously turned several pages in my book. To my chagrin, I nearly knocked it to the floor.

She laughed, a low purring sort of laugh.

I had no choice but to glance up at her. She resembled, I thought, Gina Lollobrigida.

She raised a finger to her lips, smiled sweetly, came around the table, and stuck a book under my nose. It contained a table with information about Indonesia and a card that read

CLAUDINE MARTIN
Special Consultant
C.T. MAIN, Inc.

I stared into her eyes, the same emerald color as her suit.

She extended a hand and then sat down in the chair beside mine. She whispered—which seemed natural in that hushed library—that she had been assigned to help in my training, adding that she would prepare me for my first assignment. "You're headed to Jakarta," she said in a voice that would have lured the most stalwart Ulysses to the Sirens. She reached across me and closed the book I had been studying. "No more Kuwait."

She took my hand and gently led me out to the hallway where she handed me another card. This one had a handwritten address on the back. "My apartment," she said. "Come there tomorrow at noon."

I was, quite literally, struck dumb.

She brushed my arm with her hand. "I know this must seem very strange," she admitted, "like a dream, but it happens." She started to turn as if to leave. "Tomorrow then?"

I managed a nod.

"Oh, yes. One thing more. Please don't mention this to anyone. Not even your wife."

Before that first session ended the next afternoon, we were lovers. After that, we met regularly in Claudine's Beacon Street apartment. She reinforced what I already knew about MAIN by emphasizing that we needed to keep everything that happened between us highly confidential. She reiterated on numerous occasions that I was a married man. "I'll never do anything to hurt your marriage," she assured me. "But even with your closest male friends, this must be our secret. That encounter at the library ought to clue you in to the importance of secrecy." Then she started to teach me about economic hit men.

She explained that our profession dated back to a pivotal event in the early 1950s. "I don't suppose anyone recognized it at the time, but Eisenhower's decision changed international politics from then on—forever." Unfolding a map, she described Iran as a crucial piece on the Cold War chessboard. "The country's loaded with oil, but . . . ," she pointed at the map, "even more important, look at its immediate neighbors: the Soviet Union, Turkey, Iraq, Saudi Arabia, Afghanistan, and Pakistan. Besides that, whoever controls Iran rules the Persian Gulf—Arabian Gulf if you speak Arabic—and can easily attack Israel, Lebanon, Jordan, and Syria with missiles." She went on to say that in the 1951 democratic elections for prime minister, Iranians chose Mohammed Mossadegh (*Time* magazine's "Man of the Year" in 1951), a prominent parliamentarian who promised to force foreign oil companies to share more of their profits with the Iranian people, or face expropriation. "He honored his campaign promise." She refolded the map. "The bastard nationalized Iran's petroleum assets." Then she grinned. "And incurred the wrath of British and U.S. intelligence. A big mistake."

Claudine spent the rest of the afternoon summarizing the politics of the Cold War in the Middle East. The United Kingdom and the United States, she said, shared a strong bond after World War II and also a sense of vulnerability over the threat of losing petroleum reserves to the Soviet Union. After Mossadegh nationalized oil, the CIA's director, Allen Dulles, demanded action. However, because of Iran's proximity to the USSR, President Eisenhower ruled against risking a nuclear war by launching an invasion. Instead, a CIA agent named Kermit Roosevelt, Teddy's grandson, was dispatched with several million dollars. He hired a band of thugs to disrupt the country. Riots and violent demonstrations followed, creating the impression that Mossadegh was both unpopular and inept. In 1953, he was overthrown, imprisoned for a while, and then spent the rest of his life under house arrest. The CIA's choice for a replacement, the pro-oil company, pro-Washington Mohammad Reza Pahlavi, was brought in and crowned Shahan-Shah ("King of Kings").

"You're telling me," I asked when she finished, "that our CIA ousted a democratically elected head of state?"

She tossed back her auburn hair and laughed. "Of course. Surely this isn't the first time you've heard that."

I admitted that I had read about Mossadegh, and others—leaders in Guatemala, Chile, and several African countries—who had gone down in coups suspected of being CIA operations. "But," I protested, "I never really believed it. Or, if I gave it much thought at all, I figured they were real threats to us."

"Well, you're right there. Those men were real threats. We must be vigilant, always. Communism will stop at nothing. Besides, the shah delivered. He welcomed our oil companies with open arms. And awarded thousands of lucrative contracts to U.S. corporations."

We discussed the broader implications, that Kermit Roosevelt's gambit reshaped Middle Eastern history and at the same time rendered obsolete all the old strategies for empire building. Washington learned that one man with a few million dollars could accomplish a task that previously had been left to armies and had cost billions. Roosevelt had transformed Iran into a U.S. puppet, and he had done it without risking a war with Russia—or, for that matter, without most of the world, including U.S. citizens, having any notion that we had brought a democracy to its knees.

"There were two problems though," Claudine told me. "First, Kermit was a card-carrying CIA agent. If he'd been caught, our government would have been terribly embarrassed, to say the least. Second, because he relied on so many untrained people, those thugs he paid, the word eventually got out. It's caused lots of resentment." She gave me a coy smile. "That's where you come in."

Washington devised a brilliant solution, one that was consistent with the growing trend toward privatization. It would hire contractors, like MAIN, to do the dirty work, rather than government employees. "And," she added, "we didn't want to rely on inciting riots. A better alternative was to corrupt officials before they ever threatened nationalization."

Claudine typically began our meetings with lovemaking, once

confiding, "You're a better student when your libido is satisfied."
But one afternoon she announced that things would be different
that day. She was dressed in blue jeans and a pullover sweater, not
one of her more revealing outfits. "Pure business today," she informed me. "This lesson is critical." She took my hand and led me
to an overstuffed leather chair. "But if you absorb it like a good student . . ." She left me at the chair and sat down on a sofa facing me.

"Time to talk about you," she said. She told me that my objective was the same as Kermit Roosevelt's: to bring countries with
resources our corporations coveted—like oil, a canal, or cheap
labor—into our fold. As a precaution against the type of situation
Kermit faced, where a leader had already defied us, I would start
by developing economic studies that justified huge loans to the
targeted country. Bechtel, Halliburton, and other U.S. companies
would be hired to build infrastructure projects. "When the country
can't pay, you demand a pound of flesh."

"That's what I'll be expected to do in Indonesia?"

"You bet. It's the reason you get paid the big bucks, fly first class,
stay in the best hotels. It's a critical country, like Iran. The main island, Java, is the most heavily populated piece of real estate on the
planet. Indonesia's got the largest concentration of Muslims in the
world, and it happens to sit on a sea of oil. It's the place where communism must be stopped, the next domino after Vietnam. We must
win the Indonesians over."

She showed me a cartoon she had clipped from a newspaper.
A wolf was rushing into a herd of elk, creating turmoil. Two other
wolves—an adult and a pup—were sitting quietly to the side.
"After your dad's terrified and exhausted them," the older wolf
explained, "we'll go in and save the day. Then we'll have our pick
for dinner."

"That pretty much sums up what we do," Claudine said. She

handed me two books: *A Theory of the Consumption Function* and *Capitalism and Freedom*. "This week's reading. Not exactly James Bond."

I perused their covers. Both were by Milton Friedman.

"But if you understand them," she continued, "you'll get to live like James Bond . . . without, of course, the pens that convert to missiles."

Those books introduced me to the theories I would apply in many Third World countries during the next decade. Thanks to Claudine and Milton, I grew proficient at my job. My life did begin to resemble Bond's, at least as far as the hotels, booze, and women were concerned. I was made chief economist. I headed up a staff of highly skilled economists, financial analysts, management consultants, regional planners, and even a sociologist, and I became the firm's youngest partner in its one-hundred-year history.

Looking back, I see that I was (as Panama's Omar Torrijos said) hoodwinked. I bought into the deception that massive loans invested into heavily capitalized infrastructure projects, combined with privatization, would alleviate poverty. But, while those loans and projects appeared good on paper, showing that the countries receiving them enjoyed economic growth, the part that was not disclosed was that paying off the interest meant diverting funds from health care, education, and other social services. The heavy debts drove more and more people into poverty and widened the gap between rich and poor. All the studies neglected to indicate that in the Third World, most of the poor live outside the statistically measurable economy. They cannot afford to buy electricity or cars, and they do not use ports and airports. The few who are hired by modern industrial parks often suffer from horrid working conditions, low pay, and high turnover rates. My job, as I would discover, was to hoodwink the world.

I came to realize that in the Third World I was both the wolf who drove the elk herd into a frenzy and the one rushing in for the kill.

I had no idea at that time that the United States shares something in common with Third World countries, or that at home I was one of the elks. Along with nearly everyone else. And like the victims of the wolves, we were being driven toward calamity.

CHAPTER 4

Iran and the Swirling Clouds

Returning from Indonesia, I was heartbroken to discover that Claudine had left Boston while I was away. But very soon after that I was sent on a short trip to Panama and then a much longer one to Iran.[1] Both countries would have a major impact on me personally. However, at first I was particularly impressed by Iran. It was a place I had dreamed about ever since reading Rumi in high school. Claudine's accounts of intrigue around Mossadegh and the shah had steeped an even deeper interest.

During the 1970s I traveled there many times as part of a team of foreign consultants charged with supporting the shah and convincing him to invest his oil revenues in projects that our corporations designed, managed, and constructed. Being persuasive with potentates whose treasuries overflowed with petrodollars was different from coercing the heads of state of countries like Indonesia to use their undeveloped petroleum resources as collateral against loans, but the end result was pretty much the same. Wine them, dine them, hook them, and reel them into the fold.

I helped induce the shah's people to "Americanize" their country, hiring corporations ranging from the biggest—General Electric, Boeing, IBM, and Citibank—to the small innovative firms coming out of Berkeley and Cambridge that specialized in new high-tech fields. Like many others, we at MAIN ignored the mounting unrest, the signs that the shah's brutal dictatorship was turning his former supporters against him, and us.

For me, this refusal to read the signs of the impending eruption lasted nearly a decade. Then suddenly everything changed.

One evening in 1978, while I was sitting at the luxurious bar in the Hotel InterContinental Tehran, I was contacted by an Iranian friend I had not seen since my college days. He had been hired to convince me to leave Iran. Quickly. Both of us were on the next flight to Rome.[2]

Two days later, news came of bombings and riots. Ayatollah Khomeini and the mullahs had begun their offensive. Over the next months, the shah fled, was diagnosed with cancer, took refuge in Egypt and Panama, and died. The mullahs railed against U.S. imperialism, calling Kermit Roosevelt "Satan's agent" and accusing Washington of "crimes against the Iranian people and humanity." Their followers stormed the U.S. Embassy in Tehran, took fifty-two Americans hostage, and held them for 444 days. Most U.S. businesses were locked out of Iran for three decades.

"There's no doubt that the 1979 Islamic Revolution was rooted in the 1953 coup," former CIA agent Bob Baer told me. A lauded operative (awarded the CIA's Career Intelligence Medal), Bob did not look much like George Clooney, the actor who played him in the 2005 Academy Award–winning movie *Syriana* that was based on Bob's books *See No Evil* and *Sleeping with the Devil*. Bob was handsome but not in Clooney's attention-luring manner. Bob and I were drinking beers at a South Florida tiki bar one Sunday afternoon in 2007. He was in the process of completing *The Devil We Know: Dealing with the New Iranian Superpower*, and Iran was very much on his mind. "Kermit impacted the entire region—and the world. I think we can safely say that there's a direct line from him, through the shah and the Islamic Revolution, to Al Qaeda."

We talked that afternoon about how different the Middle East might look now if we had supported Mossadegh instead of over-throwing him, and how encouraging the democratically elected prime minister to use oil money to elevate Iran's people from the extreme poverty they suffered would have established a far better model than the one offered by the shah. The conflicts between Sunnis and Shi'ia and Arabs and Israelis might have been resolved long ago had we respected democracy and allowed the region to use its considerable resources to alleviate poverty and suffering.

"I'm worried," Bob added, "that 1953 will continue to haunt any progressive candidates who run for prime minister in the next elections."

The June 2009 Iranian elections were viewed by the Obama administration, the U.S. Congress, and many corporate heads as offering hope for regime change. Instead, Bob's fears materialized. The world watched Iran tear itself apart. Every time I read another article about the riots and the police brutality, I thought about Kermit Roosevelt. The leaders in Iran who defended as legitimate the election of the conservative incumbent favorite of the mullahs, Mahmoud Ahmadinejad, over the more pro-western Mir Hossein Mousavi cited the CIA coup against Mossadegh as a reason not to bow to U.S. pressures or cooperate with Washington.

It seems that Iran is a warning to us in the United States. And it has nothing to do with nuclear weapons. Iran tells us that we need to wake up to the undercurrent of discontent that surrounds us. If we make the same mistakes now that we made with Mossadegh and then throughout the shah's regime, and if we fail to read the signs here in the United States, we are likely to find ourselves facing something every bit as tumultuous as what Iran has endured. We will not be ruled by mullahs, but the impact on our society will go far beyond the economic crises that have already hit us.

The 2009 postelection events in Iran highlight the fact that the world has changed radically since that last night I was there in 1978.

Back then, the Cold War raged. There were two superpowers, but that was changing rapidly. The mutant form of capitalism espoused in those two books that Claudine had given me drove the Soviet Union off the superpower list.

For a while a single country dominated: the United States. That is now ending. The planet's geopolitics have changed. We have entered a time of realignment not unlike the one that occurred when city-states joined together to form nations. Except this time it is global; nations are becoming less relevant. The emerging rulers are not presidents, dictators, government officials, or politicians.

The rulers are corporate CEOs, members of the corporatocracy. Like huge clouds swirling around the globe, their conglomerates reach every continent, country, and village. They are unrestricted by national borders or any particular sets of law. Although many are headquartered in the United States and call upon the U.S. military to protect their interests, they feel no sense of loyalty to any one country. They form partnerships with the Chinese and the Taiwanese, with Israel and the Arab nations, with Brazilians, Australians, Russians, Indonesians, Congolese—with anyone who possesses resources they covet. As we have seen with Halliburton, they think nothing of relocating to places like Dubai, where they pay fewer taxes.

This is the world that Claudine trained me to create, the world of Milton Friedman, Ronald Reagan, the shah of Iran, and the EHM. It was never really about the United States. It was about privatization and deregulation. The mantra "good government is less government" summed it up. The ideal was always a type of "free trade" whereby the only restrictions that applied were those that favored the multinationals and the only governments that mattered were ones that would provide soldiers to guard oil wells, dams, mines, and other corporate assets. The mutant virus took the USSR off the superpower list and then it did the same to the United States.

The ruling elites—the members of the corporatocracy—bear a disturbing resemblance to the shah of Iran and those other dictators we empowered. Unlike elected presidents, premiers, or prime ministers, they are not chosen by the people, do not serve limited terms, and answer to no one (they profess to report to boards of directors, but they all serve on each other's boards and are mutually supportive). They wield tremendous influence in the halls of both local and national governments. Almost no politician gets elected without money that flows through them and their stockholders. They control the mainstream media, either through direct ownership or advertising budgets.

I want to emphasize that I do not subscribe to a conspiracy theory. These people do not have to conspire; they do not need to commit illegal acts. Many of them have never met the majority of their peers.

The figures around national campaign financing provide a blueprint of their methods. In 2008, candidates running for the U.S. House of Representatives raised $978 million for their campaigns. U.S. Senate candidates brought in $410 million while the presidential candidates raised $1.8 billion.[3] The vast majority of this money came from corporate donations, political action committees (PACs), and individual stockholders who contributed in the expectation of increasing company profits. There is nothing conspiratorial about this; yet it does invest corporations with a great deal of political power.

The same can be said for the use of lobbyists, one of the most effective political weapons in the corporatocracy's arsenal. These men and women make sure that politicians draft laws that support corporate needs, even when those laws countermand campaign promises and disregard public opinion.

Estimates of the number of lobbyists in Washington, D.C., vary, depending on congressional agendas. At any given time, there may

be from 11,000 to 30,000. American University's Center for Congressional and Presidential Studies concluded in a 2006 report that $2.13
billion was spent on lobbying in 2004. One of its Ph.D. candidates
estimated that as many as 150,000 people were working to influence
public policy, even though the majority were not legally classified
as lobbyists.[4]

In early 2009 people around the planet attempted to figure out
what had caused the worldwide financial collapse. Conclusions
presented in a 231-page report issued on March 4, 2009, by Essential
Information and the Consumer Education Foundation were summarized as follows:

> The financial sector invested more than $5 billion in political
> influence purchasing in Washington over the past decade,
> with as many as 3,000 lobbyists winning deregulation and
> other policy decisions that led directly to the current finan-
> cial collapse.... [F]rom 1998–2008, Wall Street investment
> firms, commercial banks, hedge funds, real estate compa-
> nies, and insurance conglomerates made $1.725 billion in
> political contributions and spent another $3.4 billion on lob-
> byists, a financial juggernaut aimed at undercutting federal
> regulation. Nearly 3,000 officially registered federal lobby-
> ists worked for the industry in 2007 alone. The report docu-
> ments a dozen distinct deregulatory moves that, together,
> led to the financial meltdown. These include prohibitions
> on regulating financial derivatives; the repeal of regulatory
> barriers between commercial banks and investment banks; a
> voluntary regulation scheme for big investment banks; and
> federal refusal to act to stop predatory subprime lending.[5]

It should be noted that the above refers only to lobbyists
employed by the financial sector. Those from many other in-

dustry groups—including energy, automobiles, military equipment, chemicals, pharmaceuticals, insurance, wholesalers, and retailers—collaborated closely with them.

Communications networks work in tandem with the lobbyists. Corporatocracy dominance of the mainstream media has grown steadily, paralleling the rise of Friedman capitalism. In 1983, fifty corporations controlled the vast majority of all news media in the United States. By 1992, that had been reduced to less than thirty. In 2004, only six huge corporations—Time Warner, Disney (which owns ABC), Murdoch's News Corporation, Bertelsmann of Germany, Viacom (formerly CBS), and General Electric (NBC)—owned most of the industry.[6] These conglomerates tend to favor mergers, consolidation, and bigness while opposing attempts to regulate multinational corporations. In both their news reporting and their editorials, they promote "free trade" agreements, privatization, and the other policies that have led to the current crises.

The power wielded by the corporatocracy is global and also at times highly personal. A project manager at a major U.S. utility company has a disturbing story to tell. He informed a newspaper that his plant had not started operating on schedule because the General Electric turbine arrived late. "Jack Welch [GE's CEO] called my chairman of the board," the project manager said to me, "and demanded that he fire me. He did." That information spread quickly throughout the industry; it sent a strong message that anyone who criticized GE would suffer dire consequences.

Shocking as that account sounds, it is not unusual. Such tactics are used regularly by people in positions of power, like Jack Welch. After GE bought NBC, the word went out that covering stories critical of Welch, GE, or any of the company's largest clients was tantamount to committing career suicide.[7] Unfortunately, such tactics are not limited to GE.

Corporate intimidation can take even darker forms, including physical violence. If you talk to men and women who work for Coca-Cola in Colombia, Nike in Indonesia, or Shell in Nigeria, or to the people who slaughter chickens for Tyson or reject Monsanto's GMO seeds in the United States, or to those who go down into coal mines in Kentucky or climb Chevron's oil rigs in Myanmar, you are likely to conclude that methods of persuasion can be deadly. The days of club-wielding union-busting hooligans are not over. Often such activities are contracted out to "security" firms that subcontract to local operators who hire non-English-speaking thugs, making it extremely difficult to ever trace responsibility back to corporate headquarters.

In *The Secret History of the American Empire* two U.S. citizens, acquaintances of mine, Jim Keady and Leslie Kretzu, cofounders of the nonprofit Educating for Justice, describe the terrifying harassment they encountered from Nike. When they lectured at universities and high schools around the United States about their experiences living with impoverished Nike workers in Indonesia, they were subjected to attacks on their character by corporate executives in school newspapers. This escalated to physical violence in Indonesia: They, their Indonesian driver, a translator, and a cameraman were chased one night along a dark road outside Jakarta by a band of ruffians on motorcycles.

"They surrounded our car," Jim said.

"Our driver was forced to pull over," Leslie added. "We were hustled out at gunpoint and pushed around. Our driver was severely beaten."[8]

Intimidation is not openly taught in business schools. "But," a Harvard MBA student told a group of us one night over beers in Harvard Square, "we know it is standard operating procedure at many companies." He gave us a sheepish grin. "The mere suggestion titillates. Who doesn't thrill to the idea of having that kind of power—and getting away with it?"

Members of the corporatocracy are not part of a conspiracy, but they are characterized by an obsession with winning. They will invest vast amounts of money to get their way. They also share a common goal: to maximize profits regardless of environmental and social costs. In seeking that goal, they have created an extremely unstable, unjust, and dangerous world.

How did people like that gain such power? How did the rest of us allow it? Why does society continue to put up with it? These are fair questions to ask.

CHAPTER 5

Mercenaries

"A good executive is like a loyal soldier," Professor Ashton used to tell his students in Business Management 101 at Boston University. "He's faithful to the cause, doesn't accept the job simply to earn a salary. He or she [glancing at the single female in our class—it was, after all, 1966] is driven by a sense of duty to long-term company growth."

When I took that class, and copious notes, Professor Ashton hammered home the idea that a businessperson has a fiduciary responsibility. "He is obligated," he would repeat time and again, "to serve his customers, as well as stockholders. In fact, he has a responsibility to the general populace to assure that his company operates according to the highest standards, in the public interest."

Corporations had been legally held to standards like those championed by Professor Ashton for more than a century after the founding of this country. States did not grant charters to companies that failed to prove they were serving the public interest, and they would shut down any companies that reneged on their promises to carry out their fiduciary responsibilities. Corporations were not permitted to purchase each other or to gain monopolistic positions by other means.

All that changed during what has become known as the "Golden

Era of the Robber Barons." Attitudes and laws shifted radically after an 1886 Supreme Court decision that bestowed on corporations the same rights as those granted to individuals—but without the responsibilities required of individuals. Corporations could buy and sell each other and enjoy freedom of speech (including publishing misleading advertisements), and they were no longer obligated to serve the public interest.

Then the pendulum swung back. The Great Depression, the New Deal, and World War II inspired government officials and corporate executives to enact laws and adopt attitudes that once again reflected a sense of national loyalty and service. During the 1933 to 1980 period, the idea of fiduciary responsibility shaped the ethics of many executives, government officials, and teachers like Professor Ashton.

It came to a sudden halt with the election of President Ronald Reagan and the ascendancy of Friedman economics. Armed with the belief that profit maximization was their only obligation, company officers felt justified in doing just about anything to increase their short-term bottom lines.

The focus on immediate performance fueled a disturbing new trend. CEOs adopted the self-image of superstars. If their sole purpose was to make money, they reasoned, why should they not be rewarded like the sports heroes and rock stars who were demanding a bigger share of the take from their events. Following the example of multi-million-dollar NFL quarterbacks, CEOs prospered from salaries that exceeded by hundreds of times those of the guys in the front lines.

The Irish organization Finfacts Ireland, using data compiled from the AFL-CIO, *BusinessWeek,* and United for a Fair Economy, published an article entitled "Executive Pay and Inequality in the Winner-take-all Society" in the August 7, 2005, edition of *Finfacts Ireland Business News:*

Nobody beats the U.S. when it comes to the difference in pay between CEOs and the average worker. In 2000, on average, CEOs at 365 of the largest publicly traded U.S. companies earned $13.1 million, or 531 times what the typical hourly employee took home. The corresponding ratio in 1980 was only 42, and in 1990 it was 85. As one source has put it, "In 2000 a CEO earned more in one workday (there are 260 in a year) than what the average worker earned in 52 weeks. In 1965, by contrast, it took a CEO two weeks to earn a worker's annual pay." U.S. CEOs' pay rose 313 percent from 1990 to 2003, an advocacy group UFE said. By contrast, the Standard & Poor's 500 Stock Index rose 242 percent, and corporate profits gained 128 percent.[1]

Businesspeople stopped judging themselves based on their companies' long-term growth or reputation in consumer polls; instead, the measurement of their worth became a function of the salaries and bonuses they could squeeze out of the marketplace or out of the mergers, acquisitions, and other short-term deals they struck. They transformed themselves from good soldiers into mercenaries selling themselves to the highest bidder.

My professors were adamant that, despite their contributions to industrial growth, men like John Jacob Astor (real estate, fur), Andrew Carnegie (railroads, steel), Henry Flagler (railroads, oil), Jay Gould (finance, railroads), Collis P. Huntington (railroads), J. P. Morgan (finance), Leland Stanford (railroads), John D. Rockefeller (oil), and Cornelius Vanderbilt (railroads) were to be vilified, not hero-worshipped. Yet, in 2009, it appeared their ghosts had returned.

A serious problem, however, confronted these modern barons. Their salaries, bonuses, stock options, and lavish expenses—

including their fleets of private jets—did not simply materialize like a genie from a lamp. They had to be squeezed out of something. That something was growth, or, rather, in many cases it was the illusion of growth.

Executives expanded their companies rapidly. They neglected long-term goals in favor of short-term deals that inflated the price of their stock—along with their salaries and bonuses. As the world moved deeper into the 2000s, opportunities to create growth—or even its illusion—dried up. Markets shrank. Rapidly.

The classic economic model of supply (s) and demand (d) curves teaches that when production exceeds demand, prices fall until demand increases and s and d reach equilibrium. The executives running the multinationals came up with a modification; they responded to the increasing production dilemmas (s) not just by lowering prices—the traditional approach—but by expanding markets, opening up new ones (d). They peddled their goods and services to India and Latin America. Demand shot up. They boosted production and then had to open still more markets—in Africa and China.

Many of the goods and services they sold catered to purely materialistic desires rather than meeting the real needs of feeding and clothing impoverished people, cleaning up polluted environments, or discovering nonpetroleum sources of energy.

"Trinket capitalism" was what Professor Ashton called it. He worried that ours had become an economy based to a large extent on aggressively marketing things no one really needed and that ultimately such an economy was doomed to failure. That was in the late 1960s. Over the next decades it got worse. Eventually, markets around the world approached saturation.

The superstar executives reacted in accordance with Friedman's principles. Rather than attempting to develop new products that reflected true needs, they opted for the quickest means of making more profits. They hit upon a creative solution: Expand the money supply and the consumer's ability to purchase. They invented new forms of credit, as a way of raising the *d* curve.

Individuals and companies were encouraged to accept loans that previously would never have been approved. Laws against usurious interest rates were dropped; people began to pay as much as 35 percent on their credit card debts. It did not take long before thousands defaulted, then millions. One business after another stumbled into bankruptcy.

In addition to devising new types of credit, executives also developed innovative ways to scam the public and the emasculated regulatory agencies. One of the most widely publicized of these was the "special-purpose entity" (SPE) created by Enron.

When I was CEO of an energy company during the 1980s and then a consultant to Stone & Webster Engineering Corporation in the 1990s, I frequently met with other energy company executives. We would start the day lounging in a boardroom, sipping coffee and exchanging industry gossip. The conversation often turned to Enron.

"Can you believe the contract they just signed in India?" someone would ask.

Or: "How about that Brazilian project?"

We all marveled at Enron's ability to strike mammoth deals that seemed "too good to be true." No one outside the company could fathom how it operated. Enron executives and consultants gave us condescending smiles. When pressed, an insider might brag about "creative financing," "innovative management," and "special relationships with the Bushes" and other power brokers.

"We're a unique company," managing director of investor relations Paula Rieker told a conference I attended. "We find the best and the brightest people, and we offer them incentives to develop the greatest and most inventive projects possible."

"Inventive" was the key. After the company collapsed, we discovered that it had invented an illusion. The SPEs appeared profitable because they were offshore units that avoided taxation and sold assets to each other at much higher prices than any legitimate market would bear. They also granted anonymity and a freedom in currency movements that hid company losses "off balance sheet." Corporate officers performed contorted financial deceptions in order to promote the impression of billions in profits while the company was hemorrhaging money.

Enron filed for bankruptcy on December 2, 2001. CEO Kenneth Lay was convicted on May 25, 2006, on ten counts of securities fraud and related charges. Paula Rieker pleaded guilty in federal court to a criminal insider trading charge.

Arthur Andersen, back then one of the five largest and most respected accounting firms in the world, bought into Enron's spiral of deception—even sanctified and promoted it. As a result, in 2002 Andersen surrendered its licenses to practice as certified public accountants in the United States.

The Enron-Andersen scandal created havoc throughout world financial communities. Hundreds of thousands lost their jobs—yet executives continued to assure the world that they were dedicated to stockholder interests. Not only did the Bush administration and the majority of Congress members appear to look the other way but they also continued to promote the "free market" concepts that had knocked out the very regulations that once protected us from such shams.

We were hoodwinked. Those people gained so much power, and we let them get away with it because they deceived us. And we cooperated. We fell for their propaganda. Subscribed to "trinket capitalism." Accepted the idea that they did not need to be regulated. Permitted them to convince us that granting them the freedom to operate unfettered somehow benefited all of us. Then, even after we knew better, we continued to put up with them because they had us.

They had us just as they had the people of Indonesia, Colombia, and Nigeria.

They had captured and imprisoned us in a cage of debt. We did not dare stand up to them.

Ralph Waldo Emerson expressed it in the simplest possible terms in his essay *Wealth*: "A man in debt is so far a slave."[2]

CHAPTER 6

Enslaved by Debt

Ecuador's president shocked the world just before Christmas 2008. Rafael Correa, democratically elected two years earlier, a man who holds a Ph.D. in economics from the University of Illinois and was trained as an economist familiar with Friedman's theories, publicly proclaimed that Ecuador was not obligated to pay its national debt. The loans, he said, had been signed by unelected military dictators who were coerced by the World Bank, IMF, CIA, and people with my old job; therefore, his country did not have to honor them.

On December 13, 2008, the BBC announced:

Ecuador is to default officially on billions of dollars of foreign debt it considers "illegitimate," says President Rafael Correa.

Mr. Correa said he had given the order not to approve a debt interest payment due on Monday, describing the international lenders as "monsters."

The president said that some of Ecuador's $10bn debt was contracted illegally by a previous administration. . . .

Speaking in the city of Guayaquil, Mr. Correa said, "As president I couldn't allow us to keep paying a debt that was obviously immoral and illegitimate. . . ."[1]

The *Washington Post* pointed out:

> Ecuador is ceasing payments not because the oil-rich coun-
> try cannot afford to pay but because it has made a political
> decision not to.
>
> Correa has been threatening default and demonizing for-
> eign investors since his presidential campaign in 2006. Most
> recently, he has cited a presidential commission report that
> found evidence of criminal violations. . . .[2]

When I met with Ecuador's energy and mines minister, Alberto
Acosta, shortly after Correa took office, Acosta told me, "Banks that
grant loans to dictators, knowing they will finance projects that
benefit the rich minorities and hurt the poor majorities, have to accept the blame for much of what is wrong here in Ecuador—and
so many other places. After true democratic elections are held, the
elected officials must stand up for the majority."

Correa, a man who likes to leave his office in the Government
Palace and wander among his people in rural villages and city
slums, had read *Confessions of an Economic Hit Man*. He too had
been approached by EHMs. He knew the pressures that could be
imposed on heads of state. He wrote an endorsement for *The Secret
History of the American Empire,* calling it "a significant contribution
to the new universal way of searching for innovative approaches to
coexistence." Those approaches included smashing the shackles of
debt enslavement.

■ ■ ■

The equatorial sun shone down on Quito, a city that sits atop the
Andes at an altitude of 9,000 feet, as I left the Government Palace
late in the afternoon and wandered into the Plaza de la Indepen-
dencia. I headed toward the old cathedral that dates back to the

sixteenth century. Suddenly, I was struck by a memory. I sat down on a bench, overcome by a combination of déjà vu and altitude sickness. Images flashed before me from my first days as a Peace Corps volunteer in Ecuador in 1968.

Large reserves of oil had been discovered in the country's Amazon Basin. Texaco was working with government officials, especially those in the military, to convince the populace that oil would elevate Ecuador from the dark ages to the ranks of a wealthy nation. I recalled students parading through this plaza waving banners that proclaimed "Oil for the People," "Petroleum Profits to Feed the Starving," and "Don't Allow Yankee Imperialists to Imprison Us." In retrospect, it seemed that they had anticipated the disaster that was about to strike their country. Then my recollections skipped ahead a year.

"It's our oil, God's gift to the people of Ecuador," newly elected President Velasco Ibarra declared from the balcony of Cuenca's Municipal Building. "We must use this gift to make sure that the people of Ecuador reap the benefits."

Ibarra's words echoed those of the students, but they did not please Ecuador's CIA-backed army. In February 1972, the president was overthrown in a coup and replaced by a military junta. After that, massive loans flooded Quito; the government hired foreign companies to build power plants, transmission lines, highways, ports, airports, and industrial parks. In essence, the Amazon with its oil was collateralized. The people were told that the "oceans of petroleum" buried beneath their jungles were more than enough to justify all the loans.

At first the students rebelled. They understood that debt was a curse. They took to the streets. I stood on a Cuenca rooftop one afternoon observing a pitched battle in the park below between rock-hurling students and police in full combat gear. I watched in horror as a tear-gas canister exploded in one student's face. The next day, I read in the newspaper that he had died. Eventually, the resistance was broken.

The EHMs had a field day in Ecuador. The new dictator, General Guillermo Rodríguez Lara, began the process of obligating his country to the loans that would haunt Correa three decades later. Lara was an EHM's dream. He had studied at the infamous U.S. School of the Americas, a training ground located in the Panama Canal Zone for right-wing dictators and their enforcers, and he was dedicated to serving the CIA and U.S. oil companies. His nickname was "Bombita" ("Little Bomb"). His rule, and that of his successor, Admiral Alfredo Ernesto Poveda Burbano, lasted for nearly a decade, until 1979. Their policies epitomized what Torrijos so aptly defined as "predatory capitalism."

When petroleum prices fell, Ecuador's economy plummeted. Predictably, the corporatocracy had the country in its clutches. Over the next decades, Ecuador was forced to sell its oil at cut-rate prices to foreign companies, strike banana and shrimp trade deals that imposed hardships on Ecuadorian *campesinos,* vote at the United Nations in support of Washington's anti-Cuba policies, and allow the United States to build its largest Latin American military base on Ecuador's pristine coast.

As onerous as all these conditions were, there was another that was even worse. In 2000 Ecuador was forced by the IMF to convert its official currency from the sucre to the U.S. dollar. The havoc this caused to people whose few savings had been held in sucres is immeasurable. The value fell from 6,500 sucres to the dollar in 1998 to the official rate of 25,000 to the dollar on the day in 2000 when everyone was obliged to convert. Millions of people in the lower and middle classes faced impending starvation; a person who thought he or she owned a dollar's worth of sucres suddenly found himself or herself with a mere 26 cents. At the other end of the spectrum, businesspeople and foreign corporations with dollar accounts in foreign banks saw their fortunes swell overnight by nearly 400 percent. An estimated 3 million people (nearly a third of Ecuador's population) fled their country and flooded the illegal immigrant labor pools in the United States and Europe.

There was one more thing that arguably was even more devastating to Ecuador in the long run than the currency conversion: the complete and utter destruction of an immense area of fragile rain forest and its impact on the indigenous cultures that had inhabited it for thousands of years. Texaco, the oil company that arrived in Ecuador wearing a savior's halo, had shown its true colors: It ravaged the entire northern Amazon region.

Finally, legal actions were taken. As of the writing of this book, a $27 billion class action environmental lawsuit against Texaco (now owned by Chevron) for allegedly dumping more than eighteen times the amount of wastes spilled by the Exxon Valdez into rain forest rivers, destroying fragile Amazonian environments, and killing hundreds of people through illegal toxic waste dumping is awaiting judgment in an Ecuadorian court. Filed on behalf of 30,000 Ecuadorians, it is the largest environmental lawsuit in the history of the planet.[3]

Ecuador is a classic case, but it is just one of many. Over the years, unelected dictators have been placed into power through the clandestine efforts of multinational corporations, international banks, and the CIA—the shah of Iran, Suharto of Indonesia, Augusto Pinochet of Chile, Anastasio Somoza of Nicaragua, Anwar Sadat of Egypt, Jonas Savimbi of Angola, Mobutu Sese Seko of Zaire/Congo, the House of Saud of Saudi Arabia, to name a few. The citizens are not involved in making or accepting the deals these leaders sign that leave their countries awash in debt.

By the time the people become aware of what has hit them, those responsible typically have absconded with their fortunes to enjoy luxurious lives in Miami, the French Riviera, Morocco, or some other safe haven. And the citizens of their country are told by the IMF and its affiliates that they are responsible for paying back the loans.

These impacts were expressed in a recent *Foreign Policy In Focus* article:

> Like many of the victims of the U.S. subprime mortgage mess, the Ecuadorian people were the targets of predatory lending. In the 1970s, unscrupulous international lenders facilitated some $3 billion in borrowing by Ecuadorian dictators who blew most of the money on the military. After the transition to democracy, the Ecuadorian people got stuck holding the bag.
>
> Over the years, the country has made debt payments that exceed the value of the principal it borrowed, plus significant interest and penalties. But after multiple reschedulings, conversions, and some further borrowing, Ecuador's debt has risen to more than $10 billion today.
>
> The human costs are staggering. Every dollar sent to international creditors means one dollar less is available for fighting poverty. And in 2007, the Ecuadorian government paid $1.75 billion in debt service, more than it spent on health care, social services, the environment, and housing and urban development combined.[4]

An old silent movie I saw at a college film festival depicts the tragic consequences of debt:

> A farmer is seated at a table on the decrepit porch of his home, his wife and beautiful daughter beside him. He holds a pen, poised to write. A banker hovers behind the family, peering lecherously at the daughter. The farmer turns to his

wife, a questioning expression on his face. She gives him a look of total defeat. On the black screen, the words "We have no choice" appear. He bends over a paper on the table and signs his name.

The banker snatches the paper and bows to the daughter, who shrinks behind her mother. As the banker skulks away, he peers into the camera and sneers. The caption on the screen reads, "I've got that girl now. They'll never be able to pay."

The screen goes black. A caption appears: "Three months later." The banker returns to the farm. The family is huddled together just outside their door. The farmer steps forward and spreads his arms wide; the camera pans to fields that are scorched and lifeless. The farmer drops to his knees and wrings his hands. The banker grabs the daughter and leads her down the steps. Fade to black.

That movie, shot nearly a century ago, was intended as a warning. Yet people around the world continue to be coerced or seduced into taking on more debt. The sad truth is that people, even today, are literally forced to sell their daughters. On August 8, 2008, England's *Herald* reported, "Some 600,000 people are illegally trafficked into the European Union each year, the majority for the sex trade."[5] The *New York Times* continued:

As many as 50,000 women and children from Asia, Latin America and Eastern Europe are brought to the United States under false pretenses each year and forced to work as prostitutes, abused laborers or servants, according to a Central Intelligence Agency report that is the government's first comprehensive assessment of the problem.[6]

Many of the women and children are sold by indebted parents from countries whose economies have been devastated through corporatocracy policies.

As the corporatocracy knows full well, debt is a powerful weapon. The fear of being forced out of our homes and losing our cars and retirement funds, as well as the humiliation of bearing the scarlet letter *B* ("bankrupt"), is hammered into most of us from an early age. "If you don't pay what you owe, you'll be a failure in life," we are told. Individuals are shunned as financial pariahs. Nations have sanctions imposed on them. In both cases, it becomes difficult—or excessively expensive—to obtain financing in the future.

The power of debt was palpable when I talked with Joe Stevenson, a New York hotel worker, in the spring of 2009.

"My union brothers were piling into the truck, on their way to the picket lines," he told me. "I grabbed my jacket and headed out to join them. Then a man blocked my path. I recognized his face, but I couldn't quite place him. I started shaking, 'tho I wasn't quite sure why. 'You got a big mortgage on that home of yours?' he said. 'Think your wife'll stick by if you lose it?' I have to tell you I turned around, folded my jacket, and went back to work. I'm no hero. I just couldn't take that chance."

Businesspeople have known for a long time that workers saddled with debt think twice before quitting, or protesting. Policies that encourage borrowing bust unions.

President Reagan understood this. Once he entered the White House, he threw the full weight of his office behind the anti-union business leaders who had financed his campaign. In the summer of 1981, he fired more than 12,000 striking air traffic controllers; it demolished their union. Then Reagan appointed dedicated union foes to head the federal agencies that were supposed to protect the rights of workers.

According to John Jordan, president of the Washington public relations firm Principor Communications and a union organizer for ten years (interviewed in 2004), Reagan's actions "really opened the floodgates to a major effort on the part of corporate America to essentially beat labor back into a corner to a place where they haven't recovered yet."[7]

But the Reagan administration's most effective war against labor was waged through debt. Laws the president advocated deceived borrowers into believing they were getting low interest rate loans when in fact the opposite was the case: Balloon payment and adjustable rate mortgages and other technically complex loan packages were created that confused consumers. The higher overall rates made it increasingly difficult for those with credit card and home equity debt to pay off their loans. It happened to people regardless of income level.

"I thought I was sitting pretty," a noted psychiatrist in Palm Beach County, Florida, told me. "I took out a mortgage and bought a house for $1.5 million. A few years later, it was appraised at $2.3 million. I took another loan, based on the increased value, and bought myself a boat. A year later, the housing market crashed. They tell me now my house is worth about 50 percent of what I paid. My business has fallen off. I'm going to have to file for bankruptcy. I'll probably lose everything."

Laws passed as a result of the Great Depression capped interest rates and effectively protected us against "the evil banker" portrayed in the old black and white film. All that changed with a 1978 Supreme Court decision (*Marquette National Bank v. First of Omaha Service Corp*) that was used a few years later, under the Reagan administration, to overturn anti-usury laws. Beginning in 1981 with Citibank, credit card interest rates began to climb. The trend continued for the next twenty-seven years. Neither Democrats nor Republicans did anything to discourage it. By 2008 banks were charging as much as 35 percent annual interest on credit card debt. Others were charging much more, legally. The Associated Press reported (April 2, 2009):

> Payday loans are small, very short term loans with extremely high interest rates that are effectively advances on a borrower's next paycheck. They're typically obtained when a borrower goes to a check-cashing outlet or an online equivalent, pays a fee, and writes a postdated check that the company agrees not to cash until the customer's payday. Finance charges typically amount to annual interest rates in the triple digits, around 400 percent, and can go as high as double that.[8]

Our obsession with lending money and earning higher interest rates has impacted the fundamental structure of the U.S. economy. The nation has suffered under a massive exodus of funds from manufacturing into the financial sector. Because returns on stocks declined while those from loans skyrocketed, the economy flip-flopped from production to paper shuffling. The business of mergers, acquisitions, derivatives, and hedge funds rose while the auto, steel, and other industries collapsed.

We believed in the inherent goodness of business and government leaders. We accepted their advice, mortgaged to the hilt, put our 401(k)s and other savings into mutual funds, and watched our economy, and our savings, implode. It seems incredible as we look back to think that we allowed a few CEOs and senior partners in the financial world to bet huge amounts of our money, reaping tens of millions in bonuses based on their phantom profits—while we rushed headlong into insolvency.

Rafael Correa's experiences as a capitalist economist who rose to become president of Ecuador give him a unique perspective on all of this. He made an impassioned plea for change on June 25, 2009, as the U.N. General Assembly debated possible new rules to deal with the global economic crisis. Discussions swirled around a proposal for increasing aid to poorer nations, tightening regulation of financial instruments, and reforming the IMF and other multilateral institutions. Correa called for abolishing the IMF altogether. He added:

> We who want to be citizens of the world cannot understand schemes that always end up trampling and enslaving the poorest. How can we understand so-called globalization that does not seek to create world citizens, but only consumers? It does not seek to create a global society, just a global market.[9]

The schemes Ecuador's president referred to are the brainchildren of today's squadron of robber barons. Most of them make the potentates of old, the shah of Iran, and the king of Saudi Arabia look like paupers. Their stories are truly amazing.

CHAPTER 7

Modern Robber Barons

Ron's, a restaurant in Hampton Beach, New Hampshire, is just down the street from the Ashworth Hotel where I worked as a bellhop the summer after my senior year in prep school.

"This is the joint the whole world's read about," Charles said as we took our seats at a table in Ron's with a view of the Atlantic. A native to Hampton Beach and a student at the nearby University of New Hampshire, he and I had met when I lectured at his school shortly after the publication of *Confessions*. "The place where our own local economic hit man, Dennis Kozlowski, hung out with his mistress, Karen Lee Mayo. She was a waitress here, married to lobsterman Rich Locke. Everyone knew her." His appreciative whistle was soft enough that the people at the next table never raised an eyebrow. "A real looker. Could've doubled for Kim Basinger."

In my youth I wished for something that would put my native state on the map. Back then you would have been laughed out of the room if you had suggested anything as outlandish as the idea that an infamous tycoon would choose sleepy New Hampshire as the location for a couple of his conglomerate's factories, his own office, and for a romance that would bounce off the tabloids onto the pages of the *Wall Street Journal* and *Fortune*.

Charles handed me a copy of a December 2002 *BusinessWeek* article, with the following words highlighted:

With every passing month, Tyco International Ltd.'s (TYC) Leo Dennis Kozlowski looms larger as a rogue CEO for the ages. His $6,000 shower curtain and vodka-spewing, full-size ice replica of Michelangelo's David will not be soon forgotten. At the office, too, Kozlowski's excess was legendary. He was the most prolific corporate acquirer ever, gobbling up 200 companies a year—nearly one every business day—at the height of his hyperactivity.[1]

"The article neglects to mention," Charles said, "that vodka was spewed from David's penis, like piss. Or that it was displayed at Karen Lee's birthday party on the island of Sardinia, and she was by then his wife." He sat back and stared out the window in the direction of the Atlantic Ocean, shaking his head sadly. "Now I ask you: What kind of man decorates his wife's birthday party with a statue that pees vodka—a replica of one of the art world's most important icons, at that—complete with an oversized schlong?" Then he looked at me. "Kind'a makes the robber barons of the nineteenth century's Gilded Age look innocent, don't you think? And Kozlowski is one of many. There's a whole crop of CEOs out there that are just as bad, or even worse."

Kozlowski has since been indicted on two sets of charges, convicted, and sentenced to prison. But so many greedy CEOs like him continue to go free, ensconced in their multi-million-dollar mansions, paid for on the backs of their employees, customers, and the public—you and me. Charles's point was well made. The collective avarice and abuses by modern-day tycoons have left their nineteenth-century predecessors sprawling in the dust of history.

Kozlowski's profligacy is symbolic of the similarities between now and the Gilded Age when captains of industry and finance like Jay Cooke, Daniel Drew, James Fisk, Henry Clay Frick, and J. P. Morgan reigned. Like them, CEOs today wield great power in both local and national governments and live extravagant lifestyles, often underwritten by the companies they run. Tyco allegedly paid for Kozlowski's $30 million New York City apartment, the $6,000 shower curtains, and half the $2 million cost of the birthday party. It is shocking to realize the extent to which we have all been hood-winked by the robber barons of our time—and by the very governmental bodies that are charged with preventing such mistreatment. It is hard for Americans to admit that we have been so blindsided that we have, in fact, tacitly encouraged these outrageous attacks on our economic and political systems. We have placed abusive CEOs on pedestals, glorifying their excessive wealth, multiple mansions, mega-yachts, and luxurious private jets. We celebrate them like heroes, instead of condemning them for pathological actions that have turned capitalism away from its creative potentials. For several decades we have empowered these people (almost exclusively men) to create a system that is scandalously wasteful, overtly reckless, and—we see now—ultimately self-destructive.

Perhaps more than any other single factor, today's tycoons exemplify the nature of the mutant form of capitalism we have misguidedly embraced and been infected with—the exploitation of the many by the few. We laud corporate executives who take advantage of workers and consumers alike—us—who openly manipulate Congress and then have the gall to brag about it. In such an unbalanced view of economics, we accept as "natural" that the CEOs of Fortune 500 companies become as rich as the Gilded Age tycoons simply because they operate under the mantle of publicly traded companies that are supposedly scrutinized by the Securities and Exchange Commission (SEC). We fail to object when we learn that roughly half the profits made by investment banks were distributed to the senior partners—not to the employees or the stockholders. We continue to honor the "billionaires" even after we learn that many among them—such as Bernard Madoff, R. Allen Stanford,

and the hundreds of executives on Wall Street and at companies like
Enron—were complete frauds and charlatans and that the whole
system was rigged and rotten.

We often justify the unscrupulous actions of modern robber barons because they contribute money to philanthropy and the arts. Yet
in this too they are emulating a pattern that reaches back for more
than a century. Jay Cooke was deeply involved in financial scandals
that brought down Canadian Prime Minister Sir John A. Macdon-
ald in 1873, even though Cooke professed to be a devout Christian
who tithed 10 percent of his income to charity and helped build
Episcopal churches. Daniel Drew made fortunes by manipulating
stock prices, and he is credited with coining the term "watered
stock"; but he was a devout Methodist who supported churches and
founded Drew Theological Seminary, which is now part of Drew
University. Henry Clay Frick, vilified for his amoral lifestyle and
ruthless business dealings, was named by *Portfolio* magazine (now
defunct) as one of the "Worst American CEOs of All Time." Yet he
continues to be honored for his Frick Collection of European Art,
which is celebrated as one of the finest in the United States. J. P.
Morgan dominated corporate finance and industrial consolidation
during his time, brokering the merger of companies that formed
General Electric in 1892 and another amalgamation that became the
monopolistic giant United States Steel Corporation in 1901. Yet he
also raised money to finance a floundering U.S. Treasury during the
1895 recession and came to the economy's rescue again in the Panic
of 1907. Among his philanthropies, Morgan helped to establish the
Metropolitan Museum of Art in New York City (of which he was
president) and the Wadsworth Atheneum of Hartford, Connecticut.
But does that somehow justify bringing on the financial ills of the
New York, New Haven, and Hartford Railroad and for steering the
entire U.S. economy away from manufacturing and into a dangerous emphasis on finance?

J. P. Morgan set a course that has been followed by many of today's billionaires—of mergers, acquisitions, and consolidations, deals that heap riches on those who mold them but wreak havoc on competitors, workers, and local economies. These transactions empower a few individuals with control of resources and markets; the CEOs who end up at the top of the conglomerates are in positions to exert excessive influence over government officials, the press, and buying trends. Because such deals are made on paper—in board rooms, law offices, and at investment banks—they seldom produce tangible goods or services. And, as we all know, paper transactions have played an ever-increasing role in the U.S. economy in recent decades. They are a major part of the predatory capitalism that has brought our economy crashing down.

Stephen Allen Schwarzman is a direct descendent of the Morgan heritage, and, in many respects, he epitomizes this new wave of robber barons. Born just after the end of World War II, he graduated from Yale University one year after George W. Bush (both were members of the Skull and Bones society). He then went on to Harvard Business School, rose to managing director of Lehman Brothers at the age of thirty-one, and eventually cofounded and served as chairman of the Blackstone Group, a private-equity firm that focused on mergers and acquisitions.

Schwarzman enjoyed an estimated annual income of around $400 million and a net worth of more than $7 billion in 2008. He makes no attempt to hide his lavish lifestyle. With typical panache, he celebrated his sixtieth birthday, on February 13, 2007, at New York City's Park Avenue Armory. Guests included former Secretary of State Colin Powell, Mayor of New York City Michael Bloomberg, Cardinal Edward M. Egan, Sony Chairman and CEO Sir Howard Stringer, former *New Yorker* editor Tina Brown, former Governor of New York George E. Pataki, chief executive of the NYSE Group (which operates the New York Stock Exchange) John Thain, Donald and Melania Trump, and ABC anchor Barbara Walters. The evening climaxed with live performances by Rod Stewart and Patti LaBelle. The *New York Times* summed up the event this way:

> The festivities served as a coronation of sorts for Mr. Schwarzman, a billionaire several times over, an active Republican donor and chairman of the Kennedy Center in Washington whose influence reaches deep into the worlds of finance, politics and the arts.[2]

In addition to his role at the Kennedy Center, Schwarzman has served as an adjunct professor at the Yale School of Management. On March 11, 2008, he announced that he was contributing $100 million toward the expansion of the New York Public Library, where he also was a trustee.[3]

The function of philanthropy is a fascinating one. As a founder and board member of several nonprofits, I have had to come to grips with questions of integrity around accepting donations from people who made their fortunes in activities that contradict the philosophies of the organizations they offer to support. It is impossible, of course, to comprehend philanthropists' true motives, which range from assuaging their own feelings of guilt, to duping the public into believing in their inherent sense of compassion, to genuinely desiring to do good. However, from a purely economic perspective, philanthropy is inefficient. A person who has accumulated billions of dollars and in doing so has caused others to lose their jobs, closed the doors of small businesses, or ravaged the environment, and then donates a small percentage of his fortune to correcting those problems or to the arts, would have served the world far better by making fewer profits while increasing employment, supporting small businesses, and insisting that his executives practice good environmental stewardship.

Bill Gates is a case in point. Cofounder (with Paul Allen) and CEO of Microsoft, he can take credit for producing real goods, ones that revolutionized human societies—albeit by driving countless competitors and start-ups out of business and creating a virtual monopoly in desktop software. In the process he amassed great wealth. He was ranked number one on *Forbes'* list of "The World's Richest People" for more than a decade beginning in 1995. In 1999, his net worth surpassed $100 billion, inspiring the media to call him a "centibillionaire." His company's position secured, he and his wife formed the Bill and Melinda Gates Foundation, the largest transparently operated charitable foundation in the world. This philanthropic organization appears to perform a vital function, focusing on global problems that are generally ignored by governments and NGOs.

As a philanthropist, Bill Gates seems to be a man of impeccable integrity. His family had given nearly $30 billion to charity by 2008. *Time* magazine identified him as one of the one hundred people who most influenced the twentieth century and dubbed him, along with wife Melinda and rock band U2's lead singer Bono, as the 2005 "Persons of the Year." Bill Gates was named CEO of the year by *Chief Executive Officers* magazine and voted eighth in the list of "Heroes of Our Time" in 2006.

However, the Bill and Melinda Gates Foundation has been severely criticized for investing its endowment in companies that are accused of contributing to poverty in the very Third World countries where the foundation's stated goal is to relieve poverty. Such investments include pharmaceutical companies that refuse to sell their medicines to the developing world at appropriate prices and a variety of corporations that contribute heavily to pollution. The foundation's response to public condemnation of these investments was to announce a review of its policies in 2007 and then to quietly issue a statement saying that its portfolio was based on maximizing returns, not judging corporate actions.

As a young founder and CEO, Gates had a reputation for brutally beating down competitors. He and Microsoft have been attacked in many countries for business practices that at best are morally questionable and at worst illegal. Governments like Brazil's have threatened to boycott Microsoft products because of the company's ruthless tactics. Over its lifetime, Microsoft has faced hundreds of class action and other lawsuits. Antitrust litigation was successfully brought against Microsoft in both the United States and the European Union, accusing the company of monopolization, blocking competition, and (in the United States) of violating the Sherman Antitrust Act. The fine levied against Microsoft by the European Union, of $613 million, was the largest in EU regulator history.

As I travel around the United States, I often hear students pointing to Bill Gates as a model of capitalism. "I can get rich," they say, "and then donate some of my money to good causes." My response to them: "Why not run a company that concentrates on improving social and environmental conditions through its daily operations instead? That's a lot more efficient, and ultimately more satisfying."

Like the robber barons who pioneered the development of the railroads, steel, and electrical appliances, Bill Gates has made stunning contributions to technology. And yet, like them, he has played a major role in widening the gap between rich and poor. Today, when the world is so much more integrated than it was a century ago—in part because of his products—the actions of people like him have far more serious implications than ever before.

Lawrence Ellison is another high priest of high technology. His Oracle Corporation is the world's largest business software company. An avid sailor, he flaunts his wealth. His state-of-the-art racing boats have entered most major yachting competitions, including the America's Cup; he is co-owner (with music and film mogul David Geffen) of one of the world's largest and most luxurious private vessels. He collects rare cars, planes, and real estate. He received a lot of positive press when he donated $100 million to a charitable foundation; then it was revealed that the foundation was his own and the donation was made as part of a deal to settle an insider trading lawsuit arising from an Oracle stock transaction. He was further denounced for pledging $115 million to Harvard University and then reneging on his promise.[4]

Ellison's business practices have come under fire practically from the beginning. He admitted to developing a marketing and accounting strategy that grossly overstated Oracle's sales and earnings. In order to avoid bankruptcy, the company laid off roughly 10 percent of its workforce and settled class action lawsuits from disgruntled stockholders out of court.

Gates and Ellison have become household names. But perhaps no one is more famous among corporate executives and MBA students than Jack Welch, the former chairman and CEO of General Electric and a person often cited as the shining star for today's enlightened businessperson. At conferences where I speak I hear his name cited more often than any other as a model of corporate leadership, despite the fact that he retired in 2001. It always sends shivers down my spine. To me Welch is the quintessential symbol of the modern CEO as predatory capitalist.

In the mid-1970s, when Welch was a vice president at GE, he vehemently fought the state of New York and environmental agencies that tried to force GE to clean up the extremely toxic PCBs its factories had dumped into the Hudson River. He ended up forging an agreement that limited GE's liability for PCB pollution to a mere $3 million. This victory helped propel him to the top of the organization, to the position of vice chairman in 1979 and then its youngest CEO in 1981. His reputation as a hardnosed negotiator, at a time when there was a strong corporate backlash against laws that protected the environment, catapulted him to national recognition. Seldom mentioned was the fact that GE workers and their families were among those most seriously impacted by the toxic waters that flowed through their communities.[5]

GE employees nicknamed Welch "Neutron Jack" (in reference to the neutron bomb) in the 1980s because he ruthlessly eliminated employees and left buildings intact. In his book *Jack: Straight from the Gut*, he boasts that GE had around 410,000 employees at the end of 1980 and that he had reduced it to just about 299,000 by the end of 1985. Although he is credited with making the organization "lean and mean," the truth is that he put more than a quarter of his employees out of work—while his bonuses and net worth soared.

In the 1990s, Welch "modernized" GE by shifting its emphasis from manufacturing to financial services. That strategy was a major driver behind the U.S. economy's unhealthy transformation from production to paper. I tell the attendees of those corporate and MBA conferences: "If you want to honor Jack Welch, give him credit for being one of the chief architects of our current environmental and economic crises."

[In an ironic twist of fate, Welch's PCB victories in the mid-1970s came back to haunt him. The U.S. Environmental Protection Agency in 2000, after sixteen years of study, announced a Hudson River cleanup plan that would cost GE $460 million.[6] Welch retired from GE the following year.]

Next in line among America's most famous executives in recent decades is Sam Walton, founder of Wal-Mart. He is honored as revolutionizing the retail business. Today, no company in the world sells to more people than Wal-Mart. No company reaches so many corners of the planet. No company in the United States employs as many people. And no company has been more criticized by consumer advocates, environmental NGOs, community organizers, women's rights groups, and labor unions. Among the complaints: Wal-Mart's poor employee health insurance policies, outsourcing to foreign labor markets, defiance of unions, sexism, management efforts at coercing employees to vote for specific parties during national elections, and strategies to close down local businesses whose owners either join campaigns to keep Wal-Mart out of their communities or are viewed as competitors.

Sam Walton was ranked as the wealthiest man in the United States from 1985 to 1988. By the time he died in 1992, he had created a family dynasty that recalls the dynasties established by John D. Rockefeller and the royal families of Europe and Asia. Daughter Alice, sons Jim and S. Robson, and daughter-in-law Christy (widow of son John) individually consistently rank among the world's twenty richest people. Their combined wealth would almost certainly put them at the top of the list.

Michael Bloomberg may be the corporatocracy's current poster boy. After receiving an MBA from Harvard, he joined Salomon Brothers as a trader and later became a general partner. When he left the firm, he used his $10 million severance pay to create a financial information company, Bloomberg LP, that expanded to include news services, a magazine, cable network, and radio stations. He was elected mayor of New York City in 2001 and again in 2005. With a net worth estimated at over $15 billion, he is listed among the United States' ten wealthiest people and has reportedly donated around $800 million to charity and the arts. He declines to receive a salary as mayor and lives in his own home on the Upper East Side, instead of Gracie Mansion, the official mayor's residence. He also owns homes in Britain and the tax haven of Bermuda. He has often been mentioned in political circles as a potential presidential candidate.

There is, however, a shadow side of Michael Bloomberg. It includes an Equal Employment Opportunity Commission (EEOC) class action lawsuit against his company for harassment of women, accusations by labor that he busts unions, and the fact that he financed his political campaigns with an estimated $150 million of his own money, giving him a huge advantage over his opponents. He is the archetype of the "revolving door" executive, one of those powerful people like former Treasury secretaries Robert Rubin and Hank Paulson who shuttle back and forth between business, government, and banking and in the process ensure that their interests are always served, regardless of the impacts on the general economy.

The list of predatory capitalists is extensive. Among other noteworthy corporatocracy billionaires: John T. Chambers, chairman of the board and CEO of Cisco Systems, Inc.; Scott McNealy, chairman of the board of Sun Microsystems; Charles Koch, chairman of the board and CEO of Koch Industries, Inc., a conglomerate with major oil and gas facilities and the largest privately held company by revenue in the United States; Charles's brother and co-owner David Koch; Michael Dell, the founder and CEO of Dell, Inc.; and Ronald Perelman, who bought beleaguered corporations and then sold them for enormous profits (among his most infamous deals is the purchase of Revlon Corporation with $700 million in junk bonds from Michael Milken's now defunct Drexel Burnham Lambert).

All told, there were 355 billionaires in the United States (45 percent of the world's total) in 2008; they were worth more than $1 trillion.[7] One thing about most of them is clear: They do not include among their goals that of being responsible citizens willing to help the workers and consumers who enabled them to gain their riches. Although these members of the corporatocracy make a show of publicly supporting philanthropies, at the same time they quietly expend fortunes on lawyers and lobbyists who fight against pro-labor, pro-consumer, and pro-environment regulations and any laws that would force the tycoons to pay their fair share of taxes.

Those with the money and power go to great lengths to cheat the system. According to the U.S. Government Accountability Office (GAO), nearly two-thirds of the companies they own and manage do not pay any income taxes at all, despite their profitability and combined revenues of about $2.5 trillion.[8] The corpo-ratocracy's lobbying efforts have been extremely successful for its members personally—and disastrous for the economy as a whole; the percentage of federal taxes paid by corporations dropped from 40 percent of the total in 1943 to 7 percent in 2003.[9]

At the other end of the U.S. spectrum are the impoverished. The official U.S. Census reports that almost 40 million people in the United States live below the poverty level.[10] Nearly 46 million people in the United States did not have health insurance in 2007—and that figure undoubtedly rose in 2008 and 2009 due to the recession.[11]

The contrast between the extremely wealthy and the destitute is something few Americans want to talk about, and yet it is a very real contributor to our current economic demise. In our literature and movies we poke fun at "banana republics," but the sad truth is that we are perhaps the world's first non-banana-producing banana republic. When we examine the state of our economy—the shortage of businesses that produce real things that people need, the huge gap between rich and poor, the current national debt, and the ex-ploitation of the many by a very few—we see a profile similar to that in the Third World. Our overall standards may be higher; how-ever, in relative terms the similarities are shocking. And every year, things grow worse.

In terms of U.S. wealth distribution: The 10 percent at the top of the economic ladder own nearly 90 percent of stocks, bonds, trust funds, and business equity and over 75 percent of non-home real estate. According to G. William Domhoff, professor of sociology at the University of California at Santa Cruz, "Since financial wealth is what counts as far as the control of income-producing assets, we can say that just 10 percent of the people own the United States of America."[12]

The conclusion that a very few people exercise undue influ-ence over the rest of us is not a pretty one. It does not reflect the way most of us are raised to think of ourselves or our system. As the short biographies above demonstrate, that small handful of people controls technology, vital energy resources, the media, the banks, and the government. It is also shocking to realize that these people so mismanaged the system that they drove us all into the terrible economic recession we now face. They themselves would have been better off if they had hired fewer lawyers and instead doled out more money to the poor—through both increased employment and tax-supported government programs. The recipients could then have become consumers. However, predatory capitalists apparently were not capable of understanding this most basic economic principle.

And we the people went along with them. We idolized their jets, yachts, and mansions. We honored their philanthropies and their pious words. We turned our resources over to them and elected them and their advisors to public offices.

One has to wonder how a country that fought a revolution against British aristocracy allowed itself to fall so far.

In a very real sense, the modern Gilded Age of Robber Barons started with deregulation of the energy sector—about the time I chose to enter that industry after leaving the EHM ranks.

CHAPTER 8

The Coming Deregulation

"I'd have to build you a volcano to burn that stuff," an engineer who was an expert in coal-fired electric power generation told me in 1984. We were standing together at the site of an old coal mine outside Scranton, Pennsylvania, peering up at a mountain of "culm"— the tailings discarded years earlier as noncombustible waste, the last stage of the coal extraction process.

"Then build me a volcano." I was CEO of Independent Power Systems, Inc. (IPS), a company founded by an engineer, a real estate developer who put up $1 million in seed money, and me, in response to the deregulation of the energy sector.

The first step in deregulation came in the form—ironically—of a new regulation. Despite its name, the Public Utility Regulatory Policies Act (PURPA) was a movement away from regulations. It was passed by the U.S. Congress in 1978 because of the energy crises that had ripped through the industrialized world. The intent was to change the electric utility companies in a way that—it was assumed—would reduce dependence on imported oil, diversify the industry, increase efficiency, and promote the development of alternative and renewable energy.

PURPA created a market for nonutility energy producers by forcing power companies to purchase electricity from independents at the "avoided cost"—the price the utility would incur by generating energy from its normal sources (generally oil or coal). PURPA was challenged by several utilities, but the Supreme Court voted to uphold it. These decisions opened the door for companies like IPS.

Our mission was to develop environmentally beneficial power plants that earned decent returns for our investors. Although IPS incorporated soon after the 1980 elections, we did not open our offices until after the Supreme Court's favorable 1982 ruling.

The engineer scratched his head. "You're kidding."

"Not at all." I picked up a chunk of black culm. Legally classified as a "waste," it had been abandoned in piles like this one that leached dangerous toxins into the land and water. I turned to him. "Build me a volcano that doesn't produce acid rain."

He shook his head slowly, as though he thought I was crazy. Nevertheless, he—and a team of engineers—did exactly that. Utilizing a fluidized-bed technology that had been employed in Ireland to burn cow manure, they designed a boiler that—on paper—would convert culm into electricity. At that point, though, it was merely theoretical.

My job as CEO—and former EHM—was to arrange the financing. It was a major challenge, given that this was an unproven technology. I spent sleepless nights and endless weeks on Wall Street trying to convince large institutional investors to trust us with their funds.

Of the eighty-four PURPA-driven independent power companies registered in the states where we worked, all but seven folded. However, by the end of the decade we had built and were operating one of the first acid rain–free plants in the world to be powered by coal—waste coal, at that. In addition, instead of sending excess heat into cooling ponds or towers, we pumped it into hydroponic greenhouses that raised flowers year round in Pennsylvania. We filled in old pit mines with the ash from the burned culm, and we planted trees in an attempt to revitalize the land.

The six other surviving companies sold out to large engineering conglomerates. IPS was the lone exception. I like to think that my hard work and managerial talents made the difference; yet I have to confess that people in high places who owed favors to a former EHM contributed to our success.[1]

In those days, acid rain was considered the biggest environmental deterrent to burning coal; the dangers of carbon dioxide accumulation were barely discussed. In retrospect, such an oversight is shocking. It strikes me now that the oil companies were determined back then to keep information about greenhouse gases under wraps. IPS's success in alleviating acid rain was hailed by environmentalists as a major breakthrough. We set new standards for the industry. We were cited by the U.S. House of Representatives and written up in the *Congressional Record* as an example of American ingenuity and entrepreneurship.[2]

That whole experience taught me a great deal about deregulation. Although my professors at Boston University had praised the regulatory policies of Franklin D. Roosevelt, as an EHM I had been surrounded by people who favored fewer restrictions. My initial success at IPS convinced me that my professors had been misled. It seemed to me that deregulation opened the door to innovation and offered an opportunity for the small guy to compete in a larger arena.

I was in for a shock.

A subsidiary of Ashland Oil Company had built our culm-burning plant under a turnkey contract—that is, a contract that specified that the plant was to be completed for a fixed price, within a specific time frame, and according to strict performance standards. The task turned out to be much tougher than anyone had anticipated. In fact, the Ashland subsidiary failed to perform, and its management tried to break the contract. Fortunately for us, our lawyers had made it airtight. The subsidiary ended up tearing out the original boiler and hiring a German firm to build a new one. They exceeded their budget by nearly 30 percent. Ashland's CEO was livid.

Finally the plant went online. Soon after that, Ashland told us that they intended to buy us out. It was their only shot at recouping their losses. I sat in a meeting with a dour Ashland lawyer, accompanied by two burly men who did not offer business cards. The attorney informed us that they could make life difficult if we refused their offer. He gave no specifics, just droned on about the slowness of the court system. Meanwhile I had visions of a graphic scene from *The Godfather*. A Hollywood mogul who refused to cooperate with Don Corleone woke up to find the severed, bloody head of his prized racehorse in bed next to him.

Our lawyers assured us that we would probably win the court battle, but until that happened the court would close down the plant and it would not generate the income required to pay our debts. The case could be dragged out for months—exactly the point Ashland's lawyer had been making while I was visualizing horseflesh. Without the revenues from selling electricity, we would be forced into bankruptcy and lose everything.

Shackled by debt. It was a language I understood.

I took a long walk on the beach that evening. I thought about my daughter, Jessica, a tender seven-year-old. The next morning I met with my partners. We decided to sell. I called my lawyer at Chadbourn and Park.

"I think it is your only option," he agreed. "These guys play hardball."

A few days later I sat in an office with Joe Cogen, the partner who had put up the initial million dollars, and Joe's personal lawyer, awaiting a call from Ashland's CEO. Joe was a pugnacious South Florida real estate developer. About five foot four inches, he was famous among local construction crews as the guy who showed up with a baseball bat whenever they fell behind schedule. He would shake the bat in the face of their supervisor and scream, "If this job isn't done on time, I'll skin your hide!" Now he paced around the room, occasionally glaring at the phone, growling and fuming, and giving me belligerent looks. I could tell he was prepared to fight.

About ten minutes later the call came through. Joe's lawyer punched the button on the speakerphone. Ashland's CEO said, "Hello." Without another formality—not so much as "How are you?"—he stated a price. It was absurdly low.

Joe rushed to the phone. "That's an insult," he shouted. "You can take the whole goddamn project and flush it down the toilet!"

The phone went dead. The CEO had hung up on us.

Joe marched out of the room and slammed the door behind him.

I have to admit that I was terrified at that moment. I was forty-four years old and was certain that if we did not strike a deal with Ashland, I would never find another job—except perhaps on one of the construction crews that built condominiums for Joe. But there was nothing I could do except sit and wait.

Within the hour, Joe's attorney received a phone call from an Ashland lawyer. The tactic had worked. They were ready to negotiate. It turned out to be a lucrative deal for all three of us partners. Nonetheless, I was terribly disappointed. I had intended to build a career from that project; instead, I was forced out of the business.

Although IPS accomplished the stated objectives of PURPA, in the final analysis we were merely a pawn for a big oil company. They had used us to help them develop a new technology and then they pushed us aside. I have come to believe that the budget overrun was just an excuse, that they had always planned on owning the plant. Their tactics amounted to the legal equivalent of extortion. Similar things had happened to the other developers.

Joe Cogen and I had lunch together a couple of months after Ashland bought us out. He talked about cowboy movies he had seen in his youth. He recalled that Ronald Reagan had starred in a couple of them. "So many of those films," he said, "were about the terrible fate of people in towns where there was no law, or the sheriff was the corrupt puppet of some rancher baron. The hero would ride in on a white horse and bring order to the place." He set down his fork and stared at me. "Seems like this deregulation idea is just a justification for lawlessness. Reagan turns out to be the corrupt sheriff, not the guy on the white horse."

In lawless places, the strong and ruthless rule. A major reason for having a legal system is to protect the weak and defenseless. Whether in towns of the Wild West or modern-day Afghanistan, the absence of laws—or people to enforce them—is tantamount to assuring that might will prevail over right. I discovered the hard way that deregulation did not open the door to innovation. It did not offer an opportunity for the small guy to compete in the larger arena. It created that impression, and then used it as a means to help the strong flex their muscles.

Consumers were the ultimate losers. They ended up paying much higher prices in many states while experiencing serious shortages in electricity supplies—including blackouts that devastated many small businesses. Some communities were forced to divert tax monies from educational, health care, and other social programs so they could bail out failed power systems. The jackals had come home to roost.

The Enron scam is an example everyone knows. Another is the entire state of California. After investigating the fiasco surrounding Democratic Governor Gray Davis and the electric utility scandal in California, *The Nation* on February 12, 2001, concluded:

> Blackouts, brownouts and soaring electricity rates have defined the political landscape of California since last spring. They've transformed the phrase "utility deregulation" into

a household epithet. . . . And they've helped create a crisis
whose economic and ecological shock waves will carry deep
into the new century.[3]

Electric usage during the year running from June 2000 to June
2001 was reduced by an unprecedented 14 percent. Governor Davis
was recalled from office and was succeeded by Republican Arnold
Schwarzenegger.[4] The California economy never recovered, all because of lax or shelved regulations and emasculated enforcers.

In the end, PURPA was a boon to the big utility companies.
These once-regulated monopolies that were restricted to specific
geographic areas have expanded and become parts of mammoth
unregulated holding companies. Florida Power and Light (FPL), for
example, created the FPL Group as its holding company; it still operates in its original territory, and it also owns hydroelectric plants
in Maine, solar units in California and Arizona, and wind farms in
twenty-one states and Canada. Duke Power restructured itself as
Duke Energy; in addition to its original North Carolina operations,
it now also owns facilities in Canada and Latin America. Baltimore
Gas and Electric created Constellation Power, which according to its
website (April 2009), is "a major generator of electricity with a di-
versified fleet of power plants strategically located throughout the
United States," as well as in its original franchise area in Maryland.

IPS gave me firsthand experience with the impacts of deregulation. PURPA was, in many respects, a test case. It was followed by
a flood of laws that negated rules and regulations established during the Great Depression, and it supercharged the mutant form of
capitalism.

CHAPTER 9

The Regulation Scam

"Some industries have to be heavily regulated or they'll self-destruct," Professor Ashton used to tell us in our BU business school classes. In addition to wanting us to become executives with integrity, he hoped to impress upon us that unlimited competition is not always healthy. "Whenever a lot of capital is involved," he lectured, "too much competition can be disastrous."

The railroads were his favorite example of a business that had been thrown into turmoil by the ruthless drive of the old train tycoons to keep government off their backs. "They cheated, robbed each other and the public, and did just about everything else to win their crazy game of Monopoly," he would say, wagging his head in disdain. "The railroads were crippled—or died—as a result."

He worried that the airline industry was following the same course. "If U.S. airlines aren't heavily regulated," he pointed out, "or even government owned, as in so many other countries, if a number of them are instead allowed to compete for the same routes, with ticket prices up for grabs, it'll be disastrous."

Professor Ashton seemed to anticipate the emergence of Milton Friedman's theories and was attempting to counter his arguments even before they were made public. I know Professor Ashton was very familiar with Ludwig von Mises and Friedrich von Hayek, two economists who influenced Friedman's work.

Mises, one of the most important economists and social philosophers of the mid–twentieth century, argued fervently in favor of laissez-faire markets. Hayek devoted himself to free market capitalism. He shared the 1974 Nobel Memorial Prize in Economics with Gunnar Myrdal, and, like Friedman, he was instrumental in shaping the policies of both Margaret Thatcher and Ronald Reagan. When Thatcher was asked what economic theory most influenced her, she reached into her briefcase, pulled out Hayek's *The Constitution of Liberty*, held it above her head, and proclaimed, "This is the bible."

It must have disturbed Professor Ashton immensely that transportation, along with electricity, were the first sectors to be deregulated in the United States since the New Deal. President Richard Nixon proposed to Congress in late 1971 to open both rail and truck transportation to more lenient practices.

Gerald Ford hammered through the Railroad Revitalization and Regulatory Reform Act of 1976. Jimmy Carter lobbied Congress to pass the Airline Deregulation Act in 1978 and the Staggers Rail Act and Motor Carrier Act in 1980. Combined, these deregulation successes reversed trends that had begun in the late 1880s. In each case, they allowed competitors to undercut each others' prices. They ultimately drove many companies to ruin.

The role that liberal Democrats played in the deregulation frenzy is an indication of the influence wielded by Mises, Hayek, and Friedman. President Carter was converted by a Democratic and liberal economist, Alfred Kahn, who was considered an expert in airline regulation—and was ultimately nicknamed the "Father of Airline Deregulation." As chairman of the Civil Aeronautics Board, he paved the way for low-cost carriers from People Express to Southeast Airlines, and he oversaw the demise of the agency he headed.

Dozens of airlines folded as a result of deregulation, including People Express, Southeast, and TWA. A landslide of failures in related businesses followed: food caterers, travel agencies, parts suppliers, and others that serviced the defunct airlines, as well as those impacted by the job losses suffered by pilots, flight attendants, mechanics, and luggage handlers. Many other major companies that had prospered under the former regulated policies filed for bankruptcy, including Delta, Northwest Airlines, United, US Airways, and Continental.

Daniel Engber wrote in a 2005 *Slate* article entitled "Why Do Airlines Go Bankrupt":

Airlines almost never went bankrupt in the old days, when a federal board controlled every aspect of the industry, including ticket prices and routes. The board would also step in when an airline was about to go under. That kind of government oversight ended with the United States Airline Deregulation Act of 1978, which opened the runways to upstart competitors. . . .

Airlines seem to go bankrupt more often than any other business, but companies in other deregulated industries, like telecommunications, have followed a similar pattern in recent years. . . . In the deregulated aviation industry, airline tickets are like a commodity—since multiple carriers serve the same routes, customers will go with whoever's the cheapest.[1]

Despite the mounting evidence of the harm inflicted, the movement to dispose of rules governing businesses had many advocates.

"Deregulation is the wave of the future," Paul Priddy, MAIN's president in 1978, told a group of us over lunch. Priddy's limited-government philosophy reflected that of former MAIN president Jake Dauber. "Unrestricted business is our answer to communism. It is time for every one of you"—he waved his arms around the room—"to hop on the band wagon! Deregulate, deregulate, deregulate. . . ."

Consulting organizations like MAIN actively promoted deregulation throughout the 1970s and 1980s, as did the Brookings Institution, the American Enterprise Institute, and other Washington think tanks. If you were stubborn enough to stick to the beliefs of the likes of Professor Ashton, you were seen as unpatriotic.

In my heart I felt corporations needed legal restrictions. By the time Priddy made that statement, I had seven years of EHM experience; I knew that corruption reigned—at least among U.S. corporations working in the Third World. From a philosophical point of view, it seemed to me that in a democracy, rules were needed to defend the majority. Truly democratic elections would keep in power those leaders who supported laws that protected us from corporate abuses and economic turmoil. Any attempts on the part of corporations to lobby or bribe politicians to loosen restrictions and thereby place us in jeopardy were not in the best interests of the majority and therefore, by their very nature, were undemocratic. I once raised this idea with a group of fellow partners at MAIN. The looks I received strongly suggested that if I valued my job, I should keep such opinions to myself. My heart yielded to my head—and my professional ambition. However, it was the beginning of the end for me, one of the factors that convinced me to quit my job a few years later.

One act of congress followed another. Interstate buses were deregulated under the Bus Regulatory Reform Act of 1982. Freight aggregators in the Surface Freight Forwarder Deregulation Act of 1986. Shipping in the Ocean Shipping Act of 1984 and the Ocean Shipping Reform Act of 1998.

I often thought back to my early training with Claudine. "Something important for you to continually do," she advised me, "is to convince leaders in the countries where you work to loosen laws that govern corporations." We were walking down the promenade in the center of Commonwealth Avenue, one of the few occasions when we abandoned her apartment and ventured out into public. She was wearing a head scarf that covered most of her face and a long baggy overcoat, intended to convince anyone from MAIN who might happen by that she was a dowdy aunt from Vermont. "Let them know that their take will increase every time they cut back on rules that protect the environment, tax our corporations, or increase wages." We walked past a man seated on a bench reading the *Boston Globe*. "There's the shadow of your nemesis," she said, pointing at the newspaper. "We don't want to see the Cross Ownership Rule spread to places like Indonesia and Iran."

She was referring to the latest law to take effect in a push toward diversity in media ownership that had begun in the 1960s. These laws had come about primarily in response to the growing influence exerted by television and as a reaction against the negative impacts on news outlets caused by Senator Joseph McCarthy's "Red Scare" hearings. The assumption made by the diversity advocates was that the more entities involved in media ownership, the greater the likelihood that the American public would receive unbiased information. In 1964, the Local TV Multiple Ownership Rule had been passed. It prohibited a single entity from owning several television stations in any given market, unless there were more than eight stations within the market. The Radio/TV Cross Ownership Rule of 1970 prevented companies from operating a television and radio station in the same market. Similarly, the ownership of both a broadcast television station and a newspaper was barred in 1975.

These laws were portrayed by their proponents as contemporary cornerstones to freedom of the press. The opposition argued that restricting businesses from freely participating in an open market to buy and sell media outlets was unconstitutional. Whenever I heard politicians espouse the latter, I thought about Claudine. She was never so hypocritical as to wrap her policies in fancy principles. She wanted corporations to control the press simply because it gave them power.

Claudine's side won. Deregulation under Reagan opened the door for media companies to enjoy what amounted to monopolistic control. The first Bush administration sought to end the Fairness Doctrine, a Federal Communications Commission (FCC) policy that required the holders of broadcast licenses to present controversial issues of public importance in an "honest, equitable and balanced" manner. In *Meredith Corp. v. FCC* (1987), the courts ruled that the FCC was not responsible for regulating the Fairness Doctrine; the doctrine was abolished that same year. The Telecommunications Act, passed under President Clinton in 1996, led to a wave of acquisitions and mergers, to decreased competition, to a significant decline in the number of commercial radio stations, and to substantial increases in the average prices charged by cable companies to their clients.

The deregulation wave throughout the media sector has radically reduced the number of media companies. As I mentioned in Chapter 3, fifty corporations controlled the vast majority of all news media in the United States in 1983; by 2004 this had dropped to six: Time Warner, Disney (which owns ABC), Murdoch's News Corporation, Bertelsmann, Viacom (formerly CBS), and General Electric (NBC).

Deregulation in the communications industry may have stimulated the greatest public debate—at least in part because the media itself was directly affected. However, from the standpoint of the current economic crises, the most damaging impacts were generated by changes in the banking, financial, and insurance sectors.

Officials charged with bringing us out of the Great Depression had recognized the need for large-scale reform in the laws that govern those who manage our money. They had witnessed the terrible consequences of banking abuses, and they consequently implemented a number of regulations to prevent such things from being repeated. The most significant was the Glass-Steagall Act of 1933 that prohibited a single company from offering investment banking, commercial banking, and insurance services. It was complemented by many other regulations aimed at maintaining a stable economy.

The reforms continued after World War II. Due to concerns that the banking industry was headed toward competition-reducing consolidations, the Bank Holding Company Act was passed under President Eisenhower in 1956. It specified that the Federal Reserve Board of Governors had to approve the establishment of a bank holding company. In addition, it prohibited a bank holding company headquartered in one state from purchasing a bank in another state, and it forbid banks from participating in most nonbanking activities.

The process was reversed with the advent of the "free market" craze. The interstate restrictions of the Bank Holding Company Act were repealed by the Riegle-Neal Interstate Banking and Branching Efficiency Act of 1994. The Gramm-Leach-Bliley Act of 1999 rescinded the parts of the Glass-Steagall Act that had not already been revoked. Clinton's economic team echoed the policies of Reagan and Bush. As Thom Hartmann points out in his new book *Threshold:*

> A few weeks before Bill Clinton was to be sworn into the office as president of the United States, he was visited by Goldman Sachs CEO Robert Rubin (who had just taken a $40 million paycheck from his last year with Goldman, and would soon become the head of Clinton's economic team tasked with carrying out the "New Covenant") and Alan Greenspan.
>
> The philosophy represented by Rubin and Greenspan doesn't believe in government as a solution to much of anything other than wars and crime . . .

Governments, they told Clinton, would be replaced by economies made up largely of corporations operating outside the realm of government control. Money (capital) would be free to move anywhere in the world, although the movement of people (labor) would continue to be tightly restricted to maximize the potential for profit in any particular part of the new world marketplace. The idea of a nation as a sovereign entity answerable to its people was, in their view, quaint and outdated. People (and nations) existed, they believed, to serve economic forces, not the other way around.[2] [*All parentheses are in the original.*]

A direct consequence of these deregulatory actions was that the nation's largest banks purchased others. Mergers followed buyouts, and one consolidation after another occurred. The most notorious of these were the marriage of Citibank and Travelers Group, an insurance company, and the merging of BankAmerica Corp. with NationsBank Corporation, which then became Bank of America and bought out the seventh-largest bank in the United States, FleetBoston Financial, and the credit card giant MBNA. Such consolidations would have been impossible under Glass-Steagall. They ended up haunting the administrations of both George W. Bush and Barack Obama.

"When Ronnie Reagan slid off his white horse," Joe Cogen told me during the lunch we shared after we sold our company to Ashland Oil, "and pinned on the corrupt sheriff's star, he opened the jail cell doors and released crooks and panhandlers. They're the high-class types, wearing coats and ties, like the Ashland CEO, but don't let appearances fool you. They're just a bunch of thieves with no laws to stop them."

As I read the headlines and watched the television news broadcasts in 2009, I kept thinking about Professor Ashton. If he is still alive, I can imagine that he is not too surprised about all the abuses we the people have endured because of the demolition of this body of regulatory laws that were established to protect us. Abandoning these laws has, predictably, led to the economic tsunami we are experiencing today. As my old BU professor used to say, "Some industries have to be heavily regulated or they'll self-destruct."

Unfortunately, the push to deregulate was accompanied by a movement to legalize deceptive accounting. In their eagerness to enhance short-term profits, executives of our largest corporations devised a system that neglected to include some very significant, real costs.

The wife of one of the music world's most popular artists came face to face with the realities behind fake accounting in one of the planet's wildest and most pristine places.

CHAPTER 10

Fake Accounting

Earlier, I talked about the 30,000 Ecuadorians who filed a lawsuit against Texaco, which has since been purchased by Chevron. The company had destroyed vast sections of rain forest and the toxic wastes from its operations allegedly had killed many people and made thousands more chronically sick.[1]

"It was horrible," Trudie Styler told several of us at dinner. Trudie had just returned from visiting the site. She and her husband, Sting, were avid supporters of the indigenous people who were taking a stand against the oil company. "Like nothing I've ever seen before. Huge pools of oil that have been there for over thirty years. Birds coated in oil. Children covered with lesions and festering sores from the poisoned water. The children! So innocent, their lives ruined." She visibly shuddered. "People are dying every week. . . . How ironic that Ecuadorian citizens living on the nation's most valuable real estate are the poorest and most miserable in the country."

"And most of the consumers in the United States have no idea," Steven Donziger added. A New York lawyer, he has devoted more than a decade to this case.

That statement expresses a sad truth about so much of what is going on in the world today and the inadequacy of our accounting procedures to assign the true costs to products. Oil is a classic example of how those who sit on the resources are inadequately compensated while those who consume them are charged prices that do not begin to cover the actual costs.

Beyond the billions in cleanup expenditures, there are other costs associated with such a tragedy: the suffering, loss of human life, families destroyed, the potentials for real economic development sacrificed, and the animals and plants that are gone forever (some might have offered cures for cancer, multiple sclerosis, and other diseases).

I described the Ecuadorian case to a group of University of Wisconsin students one evening as we sat around a table at dinner.

"It raises the question," Sarah, an accounting major, said, "of what Texaco would've done if they had been forced to apply true accounting, rather than the fake number crunching we are all taught today."

"Externalities," another student interjected.

"Exactly." Sarah frowned. She glanced around the table. "The contract was between the Ecuadorian government and Texaco. The indigenous people were barred from the negotiating table."

Many costs never are taken into account when determining the price of the goods and services we consume. They are considered "externalities." They include the social and environmental costs of the destruction of resources, the pollution, and the burdens on society of workers who become injured or ill and receive little or no health care; the indirect funding of companies that are permitted to market hazardous products, dump wastes into rivers or oceans, pay employees less than a living wage, provide substandard working conditions, extract natural resources from public lands at less-than-market prices, and receive public subsidies and exemptions; the massive advertising and lobbying campaigns and the complex transportation and communications systems that are underwritten by taxpayers; and the executives' inflated salaries, bonuses, perks, and "golden retirement parachutes" that are written off as tax deductions. Since these costs do not directly impact the agreements signed by the contracting parties, they are simply ignored; however, many of them seriously impact third parties who are considered either irrelevant or too powerless to matter.

They also contribute to the current global economic crises. Because so many resources are underpriced, they are wasted casually and depleted unnecessarily. Instead of recycling or using them more efficiently, we continue to drill, mine, extract, and manufacture with reckless abandon. One of the things that most upset the people of Iceland when I was there was that the cheap electricity provided to the aluminum smelters by their government deterred companies like Alcoa from investing in recycling programs.

The Ecuadorian and Icelandic cases offer another example of how the mutant form of capitalism we have embraced has wreaked havoc on our economy. The mantra that the only responsibility of business is to make short-term profits has created an unrealistic and false set of accounting principles.

Future generations, looking back, will hold us responsible for passing the costs on to them of forests devastated during oil operations, resources depleted, and hundreds of other factors that are conveniently ignored as "externalities." For it is our children and grandchildren who will be left holding the bills.

Proponents of this sort of deceptive accounting maintain that there is no alternative, that we cannot measure such factors. But that simply is not true.

"We have to estimate the values for some of these costs," Sarah admitted. "But accountants do that all the time. Our system of depreciation is based on estimated life expectancies. So too is the 'amortization' of intangible assets like goodwill and the value of patents and trademarks. We can certainly arrive at a rational approach for quantifying the externalities, one that presents a level playing field for all participants. It is better to err somewhat in our estimates than simply to ignore such factors."

Sarah, along with a number of other academics and CPAs, are part of a movement that advocates *full cost accounting* (FCA)—sometimes referred to as *true cost accounting* (TCA). Such approaches require the inclusion of information about both costs and benefits for each good and service, as well as possible alternatives, before a decision is made as to whether to produce and market it. Charges for these should include:

1. All visible costs (not simply the immediate cash outlays)

2. Hidden costs (such as those incurred in the Ecuadorian Amazon)

3. Overhead and indirect costs (including research and development, public relations, management salaries and bonuses)

4. Past and future costs (for example, feeding the families of workers who died from asphyxiation in a Congo mine so the world could have cheap coltan for cell phones and computers and providing for people who will need health care because of horrible working conditions in an Indonesian sweatshop)

5. Life cycle costs (valuation of the environmental and social impacts of a given product or service necessitated by its existence and its disposal)

The irony is that if these costs were included, the entire world would be better off. Under FCA, the goods and services provided in the most socially and environmentally responsible manner would undoubtedly also be the least expensive. In a true "free market" economy, consumers would pay a premium for products that strain the economy and society; the price would include costs for correcting the damage. Those goods and services that are inherently "clean" would also be the cheapest.

Many corporations pay lip service to the idea of the *triple bottom line* (environmental, social, and economic), and some are actually introducing practices that move toward FCA. The latter reinforce the contention that such costs can be measured. Among those organizations making such an effort, the following were mentioned at the table that night during my meeting with the students in Wisconsin:

- The state of Florida claims to use a version of full cost accounting for its solid waste management programs.

- The urban ecology and industrial ecology approaches to architecture and regional planning stress the importance of treating the built environment as an ecosystem and of minimizing wastes.

- The Natural Step is one of several nonprofits that has worked with hundreds of businesses to help them establish accounting procedures that include life cycle costs.

- Interface Carpet Company is perhaps the most famous case study of how things can be changed in a big corporation.

Interface began operating in 1973 as a standard floor coverings manufacturer. In the mid-1990s, its chairman and CEO Ray Anderson experienced what he has described as an "epiphany." As a result, he shifted the company's strategy toward industrial practices with a "focus on sustainability without sacrificing our business goals." Anderson's book *Mid-Course Correction* discussed his own awakening to environmental concerns and presented a model for alternatives to "wasteful management"; it became a standard text for students and executives interested in new approaches. Interface's website states:

> Business and industrialism developed in a different world from the one we live in today: fewer people, less material well-being, plentiful natural resources. What emerged was a highly productive, take-make-and-waste system that assumed infinite resources with little to no thought given to its impact. Today, that system no longer enhances our prosperity; instead, it is endangering it. When Interface saw itself as part of this system and the collective problem, we began a journey in a different direction, toward sustainability. . . .
>
> Our journey has been incredibly good for the business of Interface. As our founder and chairman, and the leader of the Interface journey toward sustainability, Ray Anderson, has said:
>
>> Costs are down, not up, dispelling a myth and exposing the false choice between the economy and the environment, products are the best they have ever been, because sustainable design has provided an unexpected wellspring of innovation, people are galvanized around a shared higher purpose, better people are applying, the best people are staying and working with a purpose, the goodwill in the marketplace generated by our focus on sustainability far exceeds that which any amount of advertising or marketing expenditure could have generated—this company believes it has found a better way to a bigger and more legitimate profit—a better business model.[2]

As consumers, we have grown accustomed to telling corpora-tions, "Give us the best tennis shoes possible at the cheapest price; we'll turn a blind eye to the sweatshop workers who are leading miserable lives, dying young, and leaving starving children behind. Sell us inexpensive petroleum for our cars: we'll look the other way when we see photos of polluted rivers and devastated forests and deserts."

The current economic crises reflect our unwillingness to "pay full price as we go." It is as though we have been, and continue to be, shopping at a huge discount mall. We purchase everything for half its price. Unfortunately our children and their children will not only have to pay full price for their merchandise. They will also have to ante up the parts we avoided—with interest.

One man who understands the dilemma facing our progeny only too well has been accused by the CIA of being a "terrorist." He is in fact a visionary, a revolutionary who stood shoulder to shoulder with gun-wielding soldiers in the mountains of Central America. He is also a Catholic priest. Today he occupies one of the most influential seats in the world.

CHAPTER 11

Double Standards

Father Miguel d'Escoto Brockmann showed me around his home outside Managua, Nicaragua. As we chatted about the indigenous artists whose paintings adorned his walls, it seemed impossible that this humble, compassionate man had been vilified by the Pope, sloshed through Central American jungles ministering to guerrilla fighters, served as a cabinet member in Daniel Ortega's government, and now was about to assume the presidency of the world's most powerful multinational political body.

The Catholic News Agency (CNA) reported:

June 6, 2008 / 12:53 P.M. (CNA)—Suspended priest and former Sandinista leader Miguel d'Escoto Brockmann has been elected to lead the next U.N. General Assembly, beginning in September of this year.

D'Escoto has been a Maryknoll priest since 1961, and in 1975 he became involved with the Sandinista movement in Nicaragua, eventually becoming the country's minister of foreign relations, a post he held until 1990.

He was suspended by the Vatican in the 1980s together with two other priests involved in the Sandinista revolution, Ernesto and Fernando Cardenal. During a visit to Central

America, Pope John Paul II publicly reprimanded him for his political activities.[1]

When Father Miguel, a fan of *Confessions of an Economic Hit Man*, learned that I was visiting Nicaragua, he invited me to join him for breakfast. After that quick tour of his home, we talked about the fact that the United States and many of the existing international institutions often preach one thing and practice the exact opposite.

"The hypocrisy of the United States and the development banks is incredible," he said as we sat down in his dining room. "Double standards. A case of 'Do as I say, not as I do.' "

We both knew that the U.S. Treasury and State departments, in collaboration with the World Bank and the International Monetary Fund purport to help Third World countries pull out of recessions; however, they actually accomplish the reverse.

"It's intentional," he said. "By driving countries deeper into crisis, those institutions cultivate circumstances that make the countries more vulnerable to corporate exploitation. What everyone missed along the line is that those steps also destabilized the global economy."

A brief assessment of the economic team President Obama assembled tells the story. Timothy Geithner (former chairman of the New York branch of the Federal Reserve and Obama's Treasury secretary), Larry Summers (ex-chief economist for the World Bank, Treasury secretary under President Clinton, and the new director of the White House's National Economic Council), and Paul Volcker (retired Federal Reserve chairman and now a top economic advisor to Obama) were some of the key architects of the double-standard policies forced on developing countries years ago.

When those nations experienced economic problems and were unable to make their loan payments, they were forced to accept "structural adjustment programs" (SAPs) that mandated that client countries drastically reduce government spending, raise interest rates (often to 30 percent or higher), privatize sectors of their economies, and sell national assets to multinational corporations.

SAPs have been severely condemned by political and social scientists around the world because they:

1. threaten national sovereignty and undermine the democratic process by transferring control to foreigners;

2. benefit the largest donors (especially the United States, European Union, Canada, and Japan) whose corporations end up owning the privatized sectors and whose financial institutions receive high interest rate payments;

3. privatize resources that had been in the public domain;

4. encourage foreign corporations to exploit workers and corrupt local officials as they lobby for lax environmental and labor regulations and tax loopholes;

5. discourage agriculture and land reform, thereby protecting aristocracies and facilitating the growth of slums and poverty;

6. increase the use of fertilizers and pesticides that damage the environment and make farmers dependent on foreign chemical companies;

7. force cutbacks on health, education, and other social services by diverting money to interest payments;

8. disenfranchise women who dominate workforces in the education, health, and other social services, and

9. cause the abandonment of women and children as rural men migrate to cities and other countries.

However, the most important criticism is that they DO NOT WORK. Or, restated, SAPs do not help the countries pull out of recessions. In fact, they drive them deeper into crisis. The proof: Geithner, Summers, Volcker, and friends—Obama's team—are urging the United States to adopt solutions to our recession that are *completely counter* to those imposed on the Third World: huge national spending programs, increased debt, reduced interest rates, bailouts, and—the antithesis of privatization—government ownership of banks, automobile manufacturers, and other businesses.

I pointed toward a painting on Father Miguel's wall where a spotted jaguar peered out from behind a wall of jungle foliage. "This double standard goes back a long time," I observed. "It's as though I told you that the best way to avoid attack by a jaguar is to quietly walk up to it and touch its nose. But when I find myself in that predicament, I make lots of noise—clap my hands and shout—and slowly back away."

"Right." He pondered the painting. "Exactly. The double standard. Or . . ." He frowned. "You tell the world that you will never negotiate with the 'Muslim terrorists' who overthrew the shah of Iran when in fact you're striking deals to provide them with weapons." He laid a hand on my shoulder. "You know what I mean?"

"The Iran-Contra scandal."

"Exactly." He touched the jaguar's nose with his finger. "You know, double standards always come back to haunt those behind them." He grinned. "We priests have firsthand knowledge about all that."

The negative impacts of SAPs were clearly defined in a letter written to the president of the World Bank, James Wolfensohn, by the Development Group for Alternative Policies on April 16, 2004. It followed an exhaustive study, known as the Structural Adjustment Participatory Review Initiative (SAPRI), begun in 1996 that involved thousands of organizations in many countries and included reports coauthored by the bank. The letter was signed by the members of the group's steering committee; they represented Argentina, Norway, Dominica, Zimbabwe, Canada, Bangladesh, Ghana, Hungary, Philippines, United States, and Europe. It began:

Dear Mr. Wolfensohn:

[W]e are writing to express our frustration and anger at the institution's continued imposition of these policies on the countries of the South and Eastern Europe in the face of clear evidence of their destructive nature and impact. Over the past decade, far from reducing poverty, adjustment programs have resulted in increased poverty and economic inequality, as well as numerous economic crises. . . .[2]

The contribution of those "numerous economic crises" to today's global meltdown is immeasurable. Ecuador is only one of several nations that has defaulted on debt payments. More are threatening to follow. Furthermore, the erosion of purchasing power in countries that agreed to SAPs drastically reduced world markets for consumer goods. Privatization led to the squandering of natural resources and escalating prices for petroleum and other commodities.

The knowledge that Washington and its allied financial institutions knowingly undermined so many sovereign nations has had severe long-term negative impacts on the United States' standing in the world. The message that our strategies are directed at exploiting rather than assisting countries has caused a disturbing rift between those who provide the resources and those who consume them. This political divide in turn plays a role in further exacerbating the economic crises.

Over coffee that morning, I told Father Miguel about a U.S. Army general who predicted the current economic disintegration as far back as the late 1970s. It was perhaps ironic that this military man was the new U.N. General Assembly president's opposite in so many respects—and probably would have killed him had he been assigned to lead soldiers into the Nicaraguan mountains. Yet that general too had seen that a fundamental weakness was infecting the U.S. system; he envisaged its consequences three decades ago, and they worried him greatly.

CHAPTER 12

Militarized, Paper Economy

"Chuck" Noble was military to the bone. A West Point graduate with a master's degree in engineering from MIT, he had served as commanding general of the U.S. Army Engineer Command in Vietnam. After retiring, he joined MAIN as a project manager. He enjoyed a meteoric rise at the company that would catapult him to the presidency, replacing Paul Priddy. Despite the fact that I had avoided the draft by joining the Peace Corps, General Noble took me under his wing. I have no doubt that he had familiarized himself with my record at MAIN and concluded that I was a loyal EHM.

A trim man and exceptionally fit for someone in (I presumed) his early sixties, he had traded his uniform for conservative dark suits. He continued to crop his hair military short, and in almost every way, he reflected his West Point training—except for one thing. He sported black engineer's boots, like the ones favored by members of the Hells Angels. Sometimes the boots were spit-polished, but usually they were smudged with dirt. They baffled me at first—they seemed totally out of character. After I got to know him, I realized that they were his way of setting himself apart—he was not a typical general, he was also a blood-and-guts engineer.

During one of his first assignments as a MAIN project manager, Noble oversaw construction of the massive Salto Grande hydroelectric facility being built near the Argentina-Uruguay border—an endeavor that would produce nearly 2,000 megawatts, create a vast lake, and flood a town of 22,000 inhabitants. At one point he arranged for me to join him.

On that trip to Argentina, I learned how much Chuck detested Communists and Socialists. He was bitter over our loss in Vietnam, blaming it on our inability to understand the communist mind, and on what he called our "weak hearts." He was determined to enlist MAIN as a vehicle for spreading democracy, which in reality meant promoting private corporations.

I learned something else from Chuck: the importance of producing goods and services that are needed by people. We walked through a Buenos Aires market together one afternoon, and he kept pointing at things he called "junk." Then he stopped and faced me. "You know," he said, "I'm really concerned that all this junk is going to bring us down. We in the States are setting an example for the world. Our movies, television, and magazines promote a false view of reality. Here we are in Argentina, and it surrounds us." He turned in a slow circle. "This stuff is pure crap. Our PR guys market it to the world, but we don't even produce it. The Japanese do—or the Indonesians. We just create the ads!"

A few months after he completed the Salto Grande assignment and returned to the United States, he sent for me. I was working in Panama at the time; I received a telex from him requesting my presence at a meeting in the Army and Navy Club. I flew to Washington and checked into my room. Late in the afternoon I joined him and two other retired generals, as well as a retired Navy admiral, for dinner.

After we sat down, Chuck glanced at the others. "I know we're here to talk about the Diego Garcia military base and the debacle in the Seychelles," he said, "but first I want to get something off my chest."

"Shoot," one of the generals said.

"Well," Chuck continued, "it's about what we in this country are doing to ourselves. Ike was a great general, but as president he coined that phrase 'military-industrial complex.' It became a dirty word. Now, my friends, this country is losing its industrial base altogether. I'm afraid we're becoming a nation of paper pushers."

"Lawyers," the general interjected.

"And investment bankers," the admiral added.

"Exactly." Chuck shook his head sadly. "I predict that before long we won't be producing much of anything at all. Just shoving a bunch of paper around. God help us."

Chuck made that prediction in 1979. Today, one can see that to a large extent he was correct. We have become a paper economy, vulnerable to the whims of lawyers and investment bankers. The trading of corporations through mergers and acquisitions and the pushing of financial paper in the form of forwards, options, futures, swaps, and other derivatives are huge parts of our system. When the economy peaked, just before the recession began in 2007, over 40 percent of U.S. profits were earned by the financial sector (although it turned out to be "paper" profits).[1] The very nature of a derivative—a financial contract whose value depends on (is derived from) the value of something else (for example, a commodity, stock, home mortgage, market index)—belies the trust conveyed by paper. Perhaps it is a sign of the times that today paper pushers seldom use paper; they do it all with the push of a button, electronically.

Chuck's concerns about the manufacturing sector were prescient. Creating junk has brought our economy down. What Chuck, who was a Milton Friedman fan, did not understand was that our obsession with profit maximization was a large part of the problem. When you view the short-term bottom line as your measure of success, you set yourself up for calamity. You believe, for example, that converting GE from manufacturing to financial services is a laudable thing to do. Or that buying low in Japan—or, today, in

China—and selling high in Buenos Aires or Minneapolis is good for the balance of payments. It does not matter that you are marketing things nobody really needs, that you are encouraging China to buy into that "trinket capitalism" Professor Ashton referred to, as long as you do it at a profit, regardless of its implications for the future and despite the possibility that in the process you may be undercutting the very foundations of our own economy.

In an article published by *USA TODAY* in December 2002 entitled "U.S. Manufacturing Jobs Fading Away Fast," the author, Barbara Hagenbaugh, pointed out:

> Fifty years ago, a third of U.S. employees worked in factories, making everything from clothing to lipstick to cars. Today, a little more than one-tenth of the nation's 131 million workers are employed by manufacturing firms. . . .
>
> The decline in manufacturing jobs has swiftly accelerated since the beginning of 2000. Since then, more than 1.9 million factory jobs have been cut—about 10 percent of the sector's workforce.[2]

Another trend has also emerged, one that gives credence to that warning by Eisenhower that disturbed Chuck so much, about a military-industrial complex. On January 6, 2004, the United Kingdom's *Independent* ran an article by Andrew Gumbel: "How the War Machine Is Driving the U.S. Economy: Military Keynesianism Might Get Bush Re-elected, But It Is Starting to Worry Economists." It included the following:

> The war has been a large part of the justification for the Bush administration to run ever-widening budget deficits. . . .
>
> The result, according to economists, is a variant on Keynesianism that has particular appeal for Republicans.

Instead of growing the government in general—pumping resources into public works, health care, and education, say, which would have an immediate knock-on effect on sorely needed job creation—the policy focuses on those areas that represent obvious conservative and business-friendly constituencies. Which is to say, the military and, even more specifically, the military contractors that tend to be big contributors to Republican Party funds.[3]

The article went on to report that during the second quarter of 2003, about 60 percent of the 3.3 percent GDP growth rate in the United States was attributable to military spending, mostly "handed out to Halliburton, Bechtel, and other private contractors." The Pentagon had, according to the author, awarded a $4 billion deal to Northrop Grumman to help develop a *Star Wars* missile defense program.

Reading that article got me to thinking about all the other industries that live off companies like Northrop Grumman, Halliburton, and Bechtel. Investments of that magnitude have many spin-offs, generating downstream profits—and profiteering—for a multitude of subcontractors. Yet, as far as I could determine, these companies were producing "expendables." Theirs are not goods any of us really need. They have one objective, to kill, and to become obsolete quickly. Such products are destroyed in warfare or outer space. Furthermore, there are not many spin-offs likely to arise from such technologies that would benefit the general population.

The article pointedly moved away from references to Friedman and back to Keynes. Was this merely another attempt at deceiving the public into believing that the Republicans were rejecting the theories they had subscribed to ever since the 1980 election, or were the Friedman advocates beginning to see a crack in their foundation?

Despite all the money poured into the military sector, the United

States spiraled further into recession in 2008 and 2009, and the manufacturing sector lost more and more jobs. On April 5, 2009, NPR's *Weekend Edition Sunday* aired the following exchange:

> *Linda Wertheimer, host:* On Friday, the Labor Department released more grim news. Another 663,000 jobs disappeared last month. That sent the unemployment rate up to 8.5 percent. This recession has been especially hard on people who work in factories. Since the recession began in December 2007, 1.5 million manufacturing jobs have been lost. Here to talk to us about the state of manufacturing in this country is Marilyn Geewax, NPR's senior business editor. First, tell us, is there a crisis in manufacturing employment?
>
> *Marilyn Geewax:* Absolutely. Factory jobs have been disappearing at a furious rate. In the past decade we've lost nearly 5 million manufacturing jobs, and last month alone we lost another 161,000. The scary thing is we know that there will be more job losses coming because the Obama administration is planning to cut spending for weapons programs. That's going to trigger the loss of thousands of jobs in defense-related industries in New England especially.[4]

The articles quoted above say a great deal about the U.S. economy and the way we the people look at it:

1. Between 2000 and 2002, more than 1.9 million factory jobs were cut—about 10 percent of that sector's workforce.

2. The Bush administration had already begun to invest heavily in military contractors during that period.

3. From December 2007 to May 2009, while billions of dollars were doled out to military contractors, an additional 1.5 million manufacturing jobs were lost.

4. And yet NPR's senior business editor was worried that there
   would be a decrease of thousands more jobs because Obama
   was cutting back on weapons programs.

What, we might well ask, does all this mean? How does it relate
to Ike's predictions? Or to Chuck Noble's?

To try to arrive at answers to these questions, it is helpful to analyze some of the data around defense spending.

The Department of Defense (DOD) announced that the U.S. military budget for fiscal year 2009 was $515.4 billion. According to the
DOD, this amounted to "a nearly 74 percent increase over 2001." In
June 2009, a study released by the Stockholm International Peace
Research Institute (SIPRI) concluded that the DOD had grossly un-
derestimated its budget—by almost $100 billion—and that the ac-
tual U.S. expenditures were $607 billion.[5] Although both of these
are staggering sums—roughly equal to the total military budgets of
all the rest of the world combined—they are deceptive in their omis-
sions since they are only the Pentagon's share of the military budget
(excluding the costs of the Iraq and Afghanistan wars).

The DOD's $515.4 billion budget (whether it is correct or off by 20
percent) covers the salaries, training, and health care of uniformed
and civilian personnel, the maintenance of weapons and facilities,
day-to-day operations, and purchases for new equipment.[6] It does
not take into account the billions of dollars spent for weapons research and development; work on nuclear warheads and reactors
under the Department of Energy; "defense-related activities" at
other agencies, including the CIA, NSA, FBI, and Homeland Security; Veterans Affairs and other mandated programs (mostly military
retirement and health care); interest on debt incurred in past wars;
the wars in Iraq and Afghanistan (which are largely funded through
extra-budgetary "supplements"); or other expenses incurred by the
military for past activities but not yet paid.[7]

When all the items in these "unaccounted-for" categories are added to the ones in the official military budget, the total exceeds $1 trillion—about twice the figure stated by the DOD.[8] It is one more example of how politicians who claim to oppose big government, taxation, and government spending manage to funnel record amounts of government money away from health, education, and other "people" programs and into the pockets of military contractors.

The United States accounts for about 50 percent of the world's total military spending, and yet the United States' share of the world's GDP is less than 23 percent. Of the other top spenders on military budgets, at least twelve are considered allies of the United States. The United States outspends Iran and North Korea by a ratio of 72 to 1.[9]

An enlightening revelation that places this in further perspective was made on May 12, 2009:

PENTAGON REQUESTS RECORD $50 BILLION BLACK BUDGET

The publication *Aviation Week* reports the Pentagon is requesting a record $50 billion for its secret black budget. This marks a 3 percent increase over last year's total. The Pentagon budget for secret operations is now larger than the entire military budget of Britain, France, or Japan.[10]

Such a huge secret allocation of money begs a serious question about democracy. How can a nation that prides itself on government "of, for, and by" the people, justify hiding such a mammoth amount of the taxpayer funds from taxpayer scrutiny?

During that same dinner meeting at the Army and Navy Club in 1979, Chuck Noble asked, "What do you think will happen to a nation that doesn't produce anything of real value?"

If we look back at World War II, an event that, along with the New

Deal, is attributed with bringing us out of the Great Depression, we see that things of real value were invented and manufactured during that time. Many of the ships, airplanes, and motor vehicles that were produced for the war ultimately were sold to private corporations or individuals. The jet engine went into commercial operation. Auto manufacturers utilized breakthroughs to produce better cars less expensively. So did farm equipment industries. Huge improvements were made in radio communications, vacuum tubes, radar, X-rays, and other technologies that opened up the mass media and computer ages. Synthetic rubber revolutionized not only tire manufacturing but nearly every other facet of industry as well, and it led to the invention of nylon and a host of new materials. Frozen, processed, and "fast foods" took off in the marketplace. Penicillin was but the first of the "miracle" drugs that totally altered medical practices. Each one of these was a by-product of the war, and each one was a stimulus to U.S. manufacturing—as well as to other sectors, including retail, services, banking, insurance, agriculture, and health care.

World War II stimulated creativity and entrepreneurship. It provided an economic stimulus that endured for many years. It should not have been so difficult for us to ask ourselves and our leaders after 9/11 how AK-47s, ground-to-air missiles, and cluster bombs would accomplish anything similar. We might have foreseen what we know now, that they would drive us into a terrible recession without the saving grace of offering anything back in return.

Chuck Noble pushed his chair back from the table when we finished dinner that night at the Army and Navy Club. He crossed one leg over the other and raised a dirty black engineer's boot until it nearly brushed against the white tablecloth. "Ever wonder why I wear these?" he asked.

"We all know, Chuck," one of the generals replied. "To hide your ugly feet."

Chuck joined the laughter. "Well, that is one reason. But beyond it . . ." He paused and shot glances around the table. "I like to think that way back in history, boots like these were invented by a military engineer. The army with the best boots won." He paused to lower his leg. "That engineer created a whole new industry. Before him, people used to make their own shoes—crude sandals and moccasins. Afterwards—well, that's progress. But it only works when the military invents things that everyone really needs."

PART II

The Solution

CHAPTER 13

Changing Capitalism's Goal

"Mr. Perkins, ... you're the most sophisticated spokesperson for corporate green-washing the corporations could ever dream of." The man was standing near the back of the packed auditorium at Regis University in Denver, shaking his fist at me. He was getting a lot of attention—and he knew it. "We want to abolish corporations."

The message was not new: *The system is broken. We can't fix it. Stop apologizing for capitalism. Tear it down. Start over.*

I peered at him across the heads of the audience. "Can I ask you: How old are you?"

A long pause. "Let's just say, the same generation as you."

"Do you really think you can get rid of corporations in your lifetime?"

I admit to the possibility of a better system, but I also do not believe that capitalism is going to fall any time soon. Nor do I think it should. Capitalism has proven to be a tremendous tool for channeling creative minds into productive uses.

I tell audiences that I have a one and a half year old grandson and I want to live to see us manifest a better world for him. In its current form, capitalism—the mutant form we have embraced—has become dangerous. That gives us reason to change it, to remake it, but not to abolish it. The new form will set more compassionate goals. Instead of maximizing profits regardless of the environmental and social costs, profits will be made within the context of creating a sustainable, just, and peaceful world.

I think that a lot of the confusion I hear from people stems from a misunderstanding of the word itself. What is *capitalism*?

> *Capitalism*, economic system in which private individuals and business firms carry on the production and exchange of goods and services through a complex network of prices and markets. . . .   —*Encarta*[1]

Like every other definition I have read, this ones does not indicate that capitalists must plunder resources and omit "externalities" from their accounting practices. Nor does it suggest that profit should be the sole motive. That the lack of regulation is a requirement. That people and countries must be burdened with debt. That the governments should not provide essential services like water, electricity, and health insurance. Or that the many must be exploited for the benefit of the few.

A brief review of history demonstrates capitalism's flexibility and at the same time gives us reason to be optimistic about its effectiveness in dealing with the current crises.

The roots of modern capitalism spring from the *mercantilism* of the sixteenth through eighteenth centuries when trading companies from Europe sent ships across the globe to expand empires and purchase goods they could sell at a profit. Organizations like the British and Dutch East India Companies were granted monopolistic powers through letters of patent. They became extremely powerful, exercising the right to raise militaries, negotiate treaties, and even dictate laws. Rulers saw these companies as the means for financing exploration. They were driven by a belief in duty to country, the conversion of "the heathen" to Christianity, and the proliferation of their particular ideas of civilization. Corporate profits funded lofty goals.

The Industrial Revolution challenged the foundations of mercantilism. Inspired by Adam Smith, in the mid–eighteenth century it shifted from a conviction that the world's wealth was a constant and that one nation could increase its prosperity only at the expense of others to a belief that additional prosperity could be created through the manufacturing process. Smith and his contemporaries expounded the virtues of a free market as the most efficient method for assuring that industrialization would maximize benefits. His classic book *The Wealth of Nations* emphasized that an "invisible hand" would guide free markets to produce the right amount and variety of goods and services. However, Smith also warned against unscrupulous businesspeople and the dangers of monopolies. In his *Theory of Moral Sentiments,* he praised the virtues of compassion. Profits were intended to finance just societies that would provide basic needs to all.

That was the theory. In actual practice, things were quite different. During the nineteenth century, the rise of factories and the mines that fed them raw materials marked the beginning of a form of human exploitation that is symbolized by images of women and children laboring for long hours under horrible conditions at boringly routine, yet often dangerous, jobs, while the owners lounged in mansions. Smith's "invisible hand" was replaced by Darwin's "survival of the fittest." Although robber barons employed every conceivable ploy to demolish competitors, in the United States they subscribed to the pretentious notion that they were agents of *manifest destiny,* a doctrine that justified the conquest of nature and the endless expansion of American territory as divinely ordained. God ordered the destruction of Indians, forests, buffalo and other species, the expansion of railroads and canals, the mining of minerals, the draining of swamps, the channeling of rivers, and the development of an economy that depended on the exploitation of labor and natural resources. The robber barons and their counterparts in Europe were simply carrying out God's will.

Such abuses stimulated a new breed of philosophers. Claiming that capitalism was inherently flawed, Karl Marx and his followers advocated a classless socioeconomic structure based on common ownership of property and the state's control over the means of production. The struggle of Communist societies to win a "Cold War" against capitalism following World War II often turned "hot"; in the end, the costs of this conflict gave communism's strongest opponents, like Ronald Reagan, their greatest power; it ultimately contributed to the collapse of the Soviet Union.

The popularity of socialist ideas in the 1930s empowered labor to organize in the United States. Unions forced the factories and mines to improve working conditions, increase wages, and offer health insurance and retirement benefits. Economic historians often cite this as an example of capitalism's ability to adjust to changing attitudes. Although the captains of industry at first opposed union demands, even violently, in the end the improved lot of workers and their ability to become consumers stimulated economic growth. By accepting some of the tenets espoused by socialist writers, artists, and organizers, the owners, as well as their workers, benefited.

The expansion of the manufacturing and mining sectors required massive amounts of capital; consequently, their owners became increasingly dependent on—and affiliated with—the financiers. Throughout the twentieth century, the individuals who provided the money—the investment bankers and brokerage houses—gained increasing control. During the New Deal and World War II, the industrialists and financiers combined forces to help pull the world out of the Depression, win the war, and establish the United States as the preeminent geopolitical power.

Entrepreneurs and executives were inspired by their wartime successes; the emerging technologies fired the imaginations of a new generation who saw opportunities to prosper by applying scientific breakthroughs to daily life. Most believed—as did Professor Ashton—that they had a fiduciary responsibility to their stockholders and the long-term efficacy of their businesses. They turned laboratory experiments into televisions, computers, and cell phones, new forms of food, more efficient appliances, and medicines. At the same time, emphasis was placed on steady, stable growth.

However, once again capitalism altered itself. The individuals who controlled Wall Street slowly replaced the captains of industry in the corporatocracy, and they subscribed to the notion that the goal of business was profit, plain and simple. With the emergence of the technology and information industries, it became clear that genius did not accomplish much without money. Companies like Apple, AOL, Amazon, and Google relied on a combination of brains and financing. Mergers, takeovers, and buyouts became the norm—always manipulated by Wall Street. Financial vehicles—paper transactions—replaced manufactured goods as the prime economic movers; giant conglomerates run by mercenary executives unseated companies that for decades had been managed by CEOs raised in the school of fiduciary responsibility.

Throughout its history, capitalism has evolved into many forms. Chameleon-like, it has adapted to changing environments. However, the current Wall Street model is unusual in the extreme. It rose to dominance after Carter lost the election to Reagan in 1980. For the first time in a history dating back more than 400 years, capitalism's goal was defined as the maximization of profits with no other motivating factors. Any attempts to rein in executives were viewed as attacks on progress.

When I hear people like the man at the back of the Regis University auditorium condemn capitalism as broken and call for the abolition of corporations, I understand that they view capitalism in this narrow context. When I hear them demand a completely new system, I find myself contemplating the failures of the Soviet Union and North Korea.

The solution to our problems is to fix the broken system, not discard it. Over the centuries, capitalism has been extremely successful at responding to the needs of the times. It has made unfertile lands productive, eradicated plagues, sent people to the moon, and resulted in untold numbers of breakthroughs in science, technology, medicine, engineering, and the arts. Today it is essential to redefine the goal. Instead of "maximizing profits regardless of social and environmental costs," the new goal could be stated as "making profits within the context of creating a sustainable, just, and peaceful world."

The adjustment is already underway. Starting more than a decade ago, "corporate social responsibility" (CSR) became a watchword in corporate board rooms. Currently every major company pays at least lip service to the idea of the "triple bottom line" (the importance of achieving social and environmental targets, as well as financial ones), and many actively seek to make it part of their culture. A wave is sweeping across the global business community.

China provides a living case study. The entire country is a laboratory. Mao tried to do exactly what the man at Regis University suggested, abolish capitalism. It was a dismal failure. Post-Maoist China, on the other hand, embraced capitalism, or what Mao's successor Deng Xiaoping referred to as a "market economy with socialist characteristics." This was a miraculous success. Today's China offers profound insights about ways to modify capitalism—as well as warnings about what not to do. Perhaps no group of people understands this better than the MBA students I hung out with in Shanghai while I was in the middle of writing this book.

CHAPTER 14

China

A Lesson in Transformation

Several times during my EHM tenure in the 1970s I stood on a hill in the New Territories outside Hong Kong and peered into China, a mysterious country I was not allowed to enter. Along with Cuba, North Vietnam, and North Korea, China was off-limits to U.S. citizens; it was locked behind a wall of secrecy. About all most of us knew was that the country was in shambles due to Mao's Cultural Revolution.

I finally had the opportunity to visit China in June 2009. When my plane landed in Shanghai, I looked through the window at the profusion of jetliners from dozens of countries and thought about all the changes that had occurred since my EHM days. China's economy had soared by unprecedented average annual rates of more than 10 percent for a third of a century. Incredibly, it was now ranked as number two in the world in purchasing power parity, just behind the United States, and number three, after Japan, in nominal GDP. I had read the statistics, yet I was unprepared for the reality behind them.

Entering the Shanghai airport was like walking off a plane into a huge glass and steel spaceship. Expansive, otherworldly. I stood

there for a moment and glanced around, overwhelmed by the sheer
size and magnificence of the place.

Images of my first trip to Asia flashed before me: Indonesia 1971,
the year before Nixon "opened up" China. The United States was
losing the Vietnam War, and we feared, as Claudine had emphasized, that the rest of the region would fall, like so many dominoes,
to Communist domination. After that trip I made dozens more, producing reports to coerce the Jakarta government into accepting massive loans to build infrastructure projects. My forecasts of economic
growth were works of fiction, intended to demonstrate that if Indonesia's leaders assumed debts that would bankrupt their nation,
they could convince their people that the investments would generate glorious returns in economic growth. We all knew that it was a
scam, that the ultimate intent was to burden Indonesia with so much
debt that it would be forced to join our sphere of influence—and
not be seduced by China. No one in those days believed that any
country could sustain double-digit economic growth for more than
a couple of years and under no circumstances for a decade.

Soon after that, China accomplished the impossible. And then
it did it again. And again. China's economy mushroomed by an
estimated tenfold. In three decades, the most populous nation on
the planet rose from the depths of poverty to become the symbol of
what human determination—and capitalism—can accomplish.

Exiting from immigration, I was met by a man with a sign that
had my name printed on it. I had expected a burly security officer
type, but he was the opposite: diminutive, shy—more like a book-
worm or computer geek than a government agent. He led me outside, past the airport hotel, which resembled another intergalactic
spaceship, and into a car. A Buick! Designed for China. Then we
were speeding down a ten-lane highway lined with billboards advertising L'Oréal, Avis, Ricoh, and Toyota—and trees.

We in the United States seem determined to focus on China's

problems. People constantly point out, for example, that its greenhouse gas levels recently surpassed ours (usually neglecting to mention that on a per capita basis our emissions are five times greater
than theirs). Driving toward my hotel in the modern Pudong district,
I was certainly aware of the low-lying mist I assumed was smog,
but I was most struck by something quite different: the profusion
of trees. There were dozens of varieties of them, everywhere. Tall,
short, deciduous, coniferous, some bursting with colors—red, pink,
white, and yellow flowers—they covered a broad center strip that
divided outgoing from incoming traffic, lined the sides of the highway, and stretched back as far as the eye could see. Many were tall;
all seemed healthy—either naturally suited to the local conditions
or pampered. Obviously planted, they were clustered in formations
that brought to mind the formal gardens of Versailles. In addition
to creating a most pleasant environment for mile upon mile, they
performed another function, that of removing carbon dioxide from
the air. It was my first inkling of China's commitment to cleaning
up its environment. When I tried to discuss this with my driver, I
discovered that his English was limited to the few words of greeting
he had uttered at the airport. I made a note to ask someone else as
soon as I had the opportunity.

"Yes," replied Mandy Zhang, an MBA student at the China
Europe International Business School. CEIBS had brought me to
Shanghai to speak at their Being Globally Responsible Conference,
and she was my host that first evening at a restaurant near my hotel.
"We are all very aware of the pollution our economic development
has caused. We young people are especially determined to turn it
around. Trees are one small part of the plan."

During the conversation, I asked her how she explained the phe-
nomenal economic growth her country had experienced.

"I've puzzled over that a great deal," she answered. "All I can
say is that we Chinese are very hardworking. And we have been

motivated." She smiled broadly. "These are exciting times. Every-one my age I know is eager to move forward into the future. Like the title of our conference says, we must be globally responsible."

"China has a long history of trading and business," fellow student Jess Zhang (no relation to Mandy) added over coffee the next morning. "We experienced a period of decline for far too long, but once the decision was made in the 1980s to get back on track, we had the resources to draw on and also the traditions."

"The west's development occurred for many, many years and included a variety of experiments," observed Joseph Yu, the conference's student organizer who was sitting next to Jess. "China could skip a lot of mistakes that had already been made. It didn't have to go through the Industrial Revolution; it jumped right into the modern age."

Although the majority of the MBA students at CEIBS are Chinese, roughly 40 percent come from the United States, Europe, Latin America, and other parts of Asia. Their school was ranked among the top ten MBA programs in the world by the *Financial Times* in 2009—along with Wharton, Harvard, Columbia, and Stanford. The conference attracted an even more diverse group. There were Communist Party members and people from Taiwan who had been raised to believe that communism was a demonic force intent on spreading an Orwellian North Korean–style model across the planet. All of the participants I talked with had spent time after graduating from college in the business world prior to enrolling in MBA schools. Many had served private corporations and multinationals, but some had worked for the Chinese state-owned enterprises (SOEs) that are the foundation of the nation's economic resurgence.

Like so many MBA students I talk with in the States, their ambitions include working toward a better world. "A lot of the Chinese students I know who received western educations are now returning to Asia," Joseph Yu told me during one of our many conversations. "We can act as bridges between West and East, helping to clear up misunderstandings and faulty perceptions. As the world shrinks and boundaries between nations blur, people like us, with cross-cultural backgrounds, have a special role. We've developed unique tools that can serve our planet and peace."

The conference lasted two days. After that the students showed me around Shanghai.

It was an eye-opening experience. Intellectually I understood that an economic miracle had struck this country, but the reality was more spectacular than I had imagined. The defining event was an after-dark cruise down the Huánpu River, Shanghai's shipping artery that divides the city into west and east, past and future. The former is symbolized by the Bund: The most famous street in Asia during the first half of the twentieth century, it was chosen by foreign powers who entered Shanghai after the Opium War of 1842 as the location for their banks, trading houses, and government buildings. Today it is an architectural museum featuring classical European, late Renaissance, Gothic, and Art Deco styles. On the other side of the river are some of the world's tallest and most glittering skyscrapers, including the Oriental Pearl Tower with huge globes that are meant to simulate pearls, the beautiful Jin Mao Tower, and the Shanghai World Financial Center, the tallest building in China. At night the contrast between old and new was especially striking; the elegantly lit clock tower of the Customs House on the west was juxtaposed in the east by an orgy of light that made Broadway look amateurish.

As I stood on the deck of our boat, Deng Xiaoping's description of a "market economy with socialist characteristics" popped into mind. I had learned from the students that while Mao is often discredited, Deng is revered as the father of modern China. In the early 1980s he decreed that Shanghai would lead the nation into an economic revival like nothing the world had ever before witnessed. The decry worked. He also proclaimed that "getting rich is glorious."

"The Chinese people, including Deng, still to this day are influenced by the ideas of Confucius concerning respect for hierarchy," Mandy said when I pointed out to her that Deng's words echoed Milton Friedman's philosophy. A cool breeze floated off the river, and an oil tanker passed by, a dark shadow among the lights, headed out to sea. "We grow up here understanding that serving our families is the most important thing we can do. Our families extend to our communities and the nation. Deng Xiaoping should be understood in this context."

It was a profound observation. If you promote the concept that making profits is the sole goal of business—or getting rich is glorious—in a culture that views the group as more important than the individual, you arrive at a wholly different interpretation of capitalism than when you apply it to a culture that emphasizes rugged individualism. The latter will look out for the greater good only when regulations mandate it, while the former will do so because the ethic is ingrained in them.

Every time I asked the Chinese students about the environment, they agreed that cleaning it up was a priority. I was told again and again that it will happen. Economic growth had been the first goal; now the time had arrived to take care of the problems that rapid development had created. During the six days I was in Shanghai, the government announced that it would levy taxes against polluters, support a company that was developing electric cars by making plug-in stations available around much of the country, and offer rebates of approximately $4,000 (U.S.) to customers who purchased those cars. "When the government says it will happen," Jess told me, "it will."

As a consequence of the recent collapse of world markets, China's economic growth fell off—to an average annual rate of increase of 6 percent in the first quarter of 2009[1] (compared to the U.S. rate of decrease of 6 percent). Judging from the newspapers and discussions at CEIBS, the Chinese are confident they will get back on track soon, regardless of what happens elsewhere. I kept hearing that the internal market of more than 1.3 billion potential consumers has barely been tapped. In addition, many people expressed excitement over the prospects of leading the world in solar energy, wind power, electric cars, and other green products.

The dean of CEIBS, Rolf Cremer, and his wife Heidi invited me to join them for dinner one evening. I figured they knew as much about the country as any foreigners since they had first moved there from Germany more than two decades earlier. "With optimism," was Heidi's response to my question about how China will respond to global economic traumas. "In many parts of the world, like Europe and the States, people complain a lot, blame others, and do little to improve things. They look for reasons not to change. Here it's the opposite. The Chinese tell themselves why it will work and swing into action—so it does work."

There is no question that capitalism has transformed China. The fact that roughly one sixth of the world's population has turned itself so totally around in three decades signals hope for all of us. China is a land of many diverse cultures—ones that throughout history frequently fought each other; it has demonstrated the capacity we humans possess for uniting in order to realize a common cause.

Rather than fearing China or criticizing its pollution levels, we can draw on its remarkable example—and encourage it to do better. It will serve us well to remind ourselves that China succeeded because it did not buy into our most recent model of more debt and less regulation; nor did it take the route of so many developing nations by accepting World Bank conditionalities and structural adjustment programs (SAPs).

I was asked on several occasions whether I preferred their centralized decision-making form of government whereby policies are mandated from the top, or our more democratic one. This question inevitably was followed by an observation that the Chinese model offered the possibility that the world might pull itself back from the brink of ecological disaster while the cumbersome nature of ours might mean that decisions could not be made fast enough to keep up with the exponential changes the world is experiencing.

At first I was indignant; it seemed a frivolous question to ask someone like me who has championed democracy. But the more I thought about it, the more I understood its very real implications—which were reinforced every time I picked up the newspaper outside my hotel room door and learned about another wall of resistance President Obama confronted when he tried to change the status quo. As I read those newspaper articles, I kept seeing examples of how democracy has been usurped in the United States. The decision-making process today is radically different from the one I studied in business school. The balance has swung from the people to the corporations. The current opposition to change in the United States is driven primarily by CEOs, their lobbyists, and the politicians who are beholden to them. The people voted in 2008 for a president who promised change and yet now the people are sitting back, watching TV, and expecting their government to take care of all the crises. Instead, their government is still catering to the corporatocracy.

So the answer to that question is that I unequivocally prefer democracy. However, I fear that our present form of government does not meet that definition. Democracy assumes an informed electorate. When a majority of the voters are kept in the dark about some of the most basic aspects of our foreign policy—the things EHM and jackals do, the lies about weapons of mass destruction, and the detention of uncharged prisoners, for example—it is difficult to claim that we are informed.

I am not in a position to say whether or not the current Chinese government is responsive to the desires of the majority of its people. I can say, however, that in the United States we have ceded many of our most basic rights to the corporations. And they have not served our best interests. They have built walls of resistance to the changes we voted for; we have done little to stop them.

Democracy is not failing us; we are failing democracy. We have allowed the corporations to co-opt the democratic process. In adopting our recent form of capitalism, we have taken a government of, for, and by the people and handed it over to the corporatocracy. The solution does not require a change in our system of governance; it simply requires a revamping of the process, along with a different approach to economics.

Capitalism's history is long and impressive. It encompasses many versions. We in the United States have been infected by a mutant strain. We experienced the resultant fevers, and now we have begun to commit ourselves to recovery. Like any virus, the corporatocracy is fighting back. We can take heart in the knowledge that we already have established an impressive record of victories. As discussed in the next chapter, we have forced our government and the biggest and seemingly most intransigent corporations to alter their ways. These past successes prove that we possess the tools for reining in the corporatocracy and winning back democracy.

David Versus Goliath

Slavery was not abolished because Abraham Lincoln found himself in the White House. It ended when the people of the United States elected a president who opposed slavery.

Women did not obtain the right to vote in the United States because Woodrow Wilson championed it. Women fought for suffrage over a long period of time, and once he became president, they launched a massive campaign to force him to support them. They waved banners wherever Wilson spoke asking why Americans should die for democracy in Europe by entering World War I when half the U.S. population could not participate in the electoral process at home.

The Vietnam War did not end because Richard Nixon was a pacifist. He withdrew our troops only after citizens across the land demanded an end to a conflict that appeared futile.

Change has always started with us.

With the patriots who threw tea into Boston Harbor in 1773. With the citizens who formed antislavery societies in the 1830s and anti–child labor movements in the 1840s. With the National American Woman Suffrage Association established in 1869 by Susan B. Anthony and Elizabeth Cady Stanton. With people who marched behind Martin Luther King Jr., and Cesar Chavez. And those who rallied with Joan Baez and Pete Seeger.

Each of those movements is part of a long tradition that included the American War of Independence. We sometimes forget that the American Revolution was a rebellion against corporate abuses that were enforced by the King of England. After gaining independence, the new government granted charters only to companies that served the public interest by expanding ports, building bridges, and importing goods demanded in the marketplace. The duration of a charter was limited to as few as ten years, or until the task for which the company had been formed was completed, and no company was allowed to purchase another.

This lasted for roughly a hundred years, until John D. Rockefeller and a few of his friends convinced New Jersey and Delaware that laws favoring wealthy investors, known as "enabling acts," would generate tax revenues for their governments—and kickbacks to politicians. Other states soon followed. After World War II, policies that ignored the public interest assumed global aspects as officials from the IMF and World Bank forced countries around the globe to privatize, deregulate, and borrow. Conglomerates purchased their former competitors; their monopolistic tentacles reached to every corner of the planet.

We have cycled through periods of our history when we allowed ourselves to be ruled by dictatorial powers, followed by ones where we took control. The period beginning about 1970 was a return—on a global level—to the earlier John D. Rockefeller–robber baron cycle. A wave swept across the country and throughout much of the world that removed power from the people, this time giving it to the corporatocracy.

During my 2009 trip to Shanghai—a city that has suffered many times from colonial and dictatorial governments—I was frequently haunted by images from those days. One afternoon I sat in the Yu Garden, a classical Chinese park developed under the Ming Dynasty, in the 1500s. I studied the twisted mountain-like sculpture, known as the Grand Rockery, that had been constructed from about 2,000 tons of rare stones fused together with rice glue. Nearly fifty feet tall, it was once the highest point in the city. Mesmerized by its peaks, ridges, ravines, and caves, removed from the bustle of the city, I experienced a sense of euphoria. Suddenly a small boy darted past me, waving a plastic sword. Immediately my mood shifted. I thought about the soldiers who forced thousands of slave laborers to lug those rocks to the city and chisel them into this fantasy world for emperors.

I too had been a slaver. I had been sent, on my first assignment as an EHM, to enslave an entire nation. I convinced Indonesian officials to accept international loans. U.S. engineering firms received lucrative contracts to build projects. Our oil companies were granted concessions to drill wherever their seismologists thought petroleum might exist, regardless of the damage to the environment and local communities. Indonesia's debt transformed the country into a virtual U.S. colony and opened the door for apparel and footwear companies to exploit workers by turning them into the modern equivalent of slaves in sweatshops. After my success there, I repeated the process in the Middle East, Africa, and Latin America. The U.S. public was duped into believing that we were helping end poverty in all those countries.

It worked so well in the Third World that we brought it home. The corporatocracy colonized its own people. It was the same approach but it was applied to individuals instead of nations: debt, privatization, deregulation. The corporatocracy knew that bringing us under their thumb always starts with us. If you manage to bury people beneath loans they can not repay and keep them entertained with sports, *American Idol,* and the sex lives of celebrities, you can control their desires and financial decisions. You can manipulate and exploit them.

Historians may well look back at September 11, 2001, as the

threshold event that ultimately exposed the weaknesses of this system. It launched the United States into a war that severely strained the economy. Perhaps more important, 9/11 symbolized our vulnerability. The World Trade Towers, icons of U.S. globalization, collapsed in a matter of minutes. The Pentagon, the brain and nervous system of the U.S. military, was not defended.

"Most people have no idea how far we've fallen," a soldier who had just returned from Iraq with an amputated arm told me after I gave a keynote address at a Veterans for Peace National Convention in Seattle. "I always thought of us as the 'good guys' until I saw what we were doing over there. We are Goliath, and now David has taken us down."

Like Goliaths, empires eventually collapse. When they do, vacuums are created. Wars erupt. A new empire emerges, usually no better—and often worse—than the former one. It is a pattern we do not wish to repeat. Instead of watching our giant society topple, let us transform it.

As a student in Boston in the 1960s, I avoided walking beside the Charles River because it reeked so badly of pollution. A river in Ohio—the Cuyahoga—caught fire because of the pollutants in it from industrial mills and chemical plants. Since then we as a nation have convinced corporations to clean up our waters. We have forced corporations to do away with ozone layer–destroying aerosol cans, banish DDT, open their doors wider to women and minorities, and stop supporting apartheid in South Africa. Recently McDonald's, Kentucky Fried Chicken (KFC), and other companies announced that they were removing trans fats from their foods—after consumers demanded these changes. As a result, trans fats were banned in some states and included in labeling laws. Electric utility companies are scuttling plans to build coal-fired power plants and turning instead to wind and solar because government agencies and NGOs are refusing to allow them to obtain permits for CO_2-emitting facilities, and their customers are insisting that they focus on sustainable forms of energy.

All these actions, like the more historical ones, started with us, the people, and were directed primarily at corporations; and after the CEOs got the message, government officials followed. The resulting changes demonstrate that the marketplace is democratic—once we decide to see it as such. It is the ultimate polling booth. Corporations exist only because we vote for them in their stores, at the malls, and over the Internet. It is up to us to decide which companies will succeed and which ones will fail.

One hundred fifty years ago we as a nation voted for Abraham Lincoln, and we fought a Civil War in defense of our principles. Later we picketed Woodrow Wilson over women's suffrage, and we held teach-ins for Richard Nixon to educate him and the country on the travesty that had become the Vietnam War. Today, we the people are called upon to speak again. When we impact bottom lines, we change stock prices and attract the attention of boards of directors. Those boards influence the decisions made in the halls of legislatures.

We the consumers have won many battles over difficult issues. Voting in the marketplace is extremely effective. Now the time has arrived to ratchet it up a notch. Now is the time to win the war and transform our "empire."

CHAPTER 16

The Burden of Melting Glaciers

You know we must win the war on the mutant form of capitalism if you cross Karo La pass high in the Tibetan Himalayas. At 16,000 feet, you look out across the barren landscape; you see the nomads tending their herd of yaks and the tiny black tents where they live as they have since before the time of Christ, and you allow your eyes to move all the way up to the glacier that blankets the nearby peaks. This ice sheet, the locals tell you, almost touched the road less than two decades ago. A child could toss a stone and hit it. Since then it has receded at an alarming rate. You shade your eyes, squinting into the glint of the sun reflected off the surface of a glacier that appears now to be at least a mile away.

As I stood at the side of the road one afternoon—somewhat removed from the rest of the group of people I had brought to Tibet—staring at that glacier, I thought about the river systems that flow out of the Himalayas: the Ganges, Indus, Brahmaputra, Mekong, and Yangtze. They provide water to hundreds of millions—perhaps billions—of people. The glaciers that serve as their wombs—their reservoirs—are disappearing rapidly.

"The people of India and China may have to wring water from stones," my Nepalese guide told me. "Literally. I've heard that the Chinese are investigating ways to convert a certain type of stone into water." He looked me in the eye and shrugged. "I know, I know.

Sounds impossible and perhaps it is. But these rivers are about to dry up. And it's all because of us. Industrialization. Global warming." He turned toward the glacier.

We stood there in silence, and I thought about how the mutant virus has attacked this place. Deregulation has done far more than simply open the door for Wall Street abuses. It has meant that we in the First World have exported our pollution all over the planet. The glaciers are melting because we have allowed ourselves to burn more fossil fuels every year despite overwhelming evidence that it is causing irreparable damage to the ice sheets of Antarctica, the jungles of the Amazon, and the glaciers of the Himalayas. And we have sent our manufacturing processes to places like China so we in the United States can breathe clean air while continuing to purchase cheap computers, tennis shoes, and appliances.

A friend of mine came to mind that afternoon in Tibet, a man who runs a highly respected environmental nonprofit in the United States. He is an avid defender of birds, animals, and national parks and a staunch supporter of laws that prohibit oil drilling off the California and Florida coasts. During a conversation he pointed out that the amount of oil available from those offshore sources is miniscule "compared to what we get from Asia, Africa, the Middle East, and Latin America." He takes a hard stance against actions that might pollute our beaches or forests and yet advocates drilling in foreign lands. The 30,000 Amazonians who watched their children die from toxic petroleum dumps and who filed the $27 billion lawsuit against Chevron/Texaco in Ecuador are testaments to the shortsightedness of such thinking.

Squinting through the sunlight at the Karo La glacier and recalling my conversation with this man reminded me that throughout history, victory in battle has sometimes led to defeat in war. Bunker Hill is a prime example. Technically the British won; however, they suffered terrible losses in terms of numbers of men and officers wounded and killed; at the same time, colonial forces learned that they had the courage and skills needed to keep on fighting. Winning environmental battles that protect U.S. beaches are ultimately self-defeating if they end up devastating rain forests in other countries. As much as we may detest the idea of oil rigs in the Gulf of Mexico, we also need to understand that seeing them from Florida's shores might convince residents of the need to conserve energy and shift to renewable sources, rather than continuing their present rate of petroleum consumption. Viewing pollution in the Himalayas or Amazon as somehow different from that in the United States is provincial and misguided.

The fact is, we are engaged in a war of survival. The only way to win it will be to focus on the global problem. The Chinese, Indonesians, Kuwaitis, and Venezuelans are not the enemy. Those who try to convince us to "stay the course," keep on consuming, find new resources and lands and people to exploit, and worry only about protecting our own backyards are the enemy. By concurring, we become their accomplices. We too become the enemy.

The guide looked back at me. "I'm afraid my people in Nepal, these Bedouin here, and yours in the United States share a lot in common."

For the first time ever, we all share a lot in common. We are confronting the same crises. Everyone on our planet is. Every life form. We are all affected one way or another by global warming, economic collapse, overpopulation, violence resulting from poverty and desperation, species extinctions, increased prices for fuels, food, and other commodities, diminishing resources, and relentless pollution of the air, land, and water.

I think about this whenever I hold my grandson in my arms. Because we are so closely linked, no child (including ones born in the United States) can hope to grow up in a sustainable, just, and peaceful world unless every child in every country has that same expectation. If the rivers of China and India dry up, the calamity will be devastating for every baby on this planet.

And for the first time in history, we are all communicating with one another. Satellite phones and the Internet reach into the deserts of Saudi Arabia and the forests of Siberia. We understand that we are under attack. The mutant virus of capitalism has infected all of us.

If we are serious about loving and caring for our children, we have no choice but to set up rules and regulations that prevent us from engaging in activities that melt the glaciers, pollute the oceans, and fill the air with toxins. Ignoring the costs to the environment of the goods we manufacture and consume is like off-loading an enormous debt from a company's balance sheet, assigning it to some fictitious overseas entity, and claiming the company's finances are healthy. It did not work, ultimately, for Enron, and it will not work for the rest of us or for Mother Nature. We have but one planet. It is our home—all of it.

CHAPTER 17

Terror and Other "isms"

Navy Seal snipers rescued an American cargo ship captain unharmed and killed three Somali pirates in a daring operation in the Indian Ocean on Sunday, ending a five-day standoff between United States naval forces and a small band of brigands in a covered orange lifeboat off the Horn of Africa.[1]

The *New York Times* published that article in April 2009. The very words "pirates," "daring operation," "standoff," and "brigands" were typical of the U.S. media; they made it sound as though white-hatted cowboys had ridden to the rescue of a town besieged by Billy the Kid and his gang. Having lived in that part of the world as an EHM, I knew there was another side to what had happened. I wondered why no one was asking about the causes of piracy.

I recalled my visits with the Bugi people when I was sent to the Indonesian island of Sulawesi in the early 1970s. The Bugis had been infamous pirates since the time of the East India companies in the 1600s and 1700s. Their ferocity inspired returning European sailors to discipline their disobedient children with threats that "the bugiman will get you." In the 1970s we feared that they would attack our oil tankers as they passed through the vital Strait of Malacca.

I sat with one of their elders on the Sulawesi shore one afternoon. We watched his people build a sailing galleon, known as a *prahu*, much as they had for centuries. Like a gigantic beached whale, it was high and dry, propped upright by rows of gnarled stakes that resembled roots sprouting from its hull. Dozens of men hustled about it, working with adzes, hatchets, and hand drills. I expressed the concerns of my government to him, intimating that we would retaliate if the oil lanes were threatened.

The old man glared at me. "We were not pirates in the old days," he said, his bushy white hair bobbing indignantly. "We only fought to defend our lands against Europeans who came to steal our spices. If we attack your ships today, it is because they take the trade away from us; your 'stink ships' foul our waters with oil, destroying our fish and starving our children." Then he shrugged. "Now, we're at a loss." His smile was disarming. "How can a handful of people in wooden sailing ships fight off America's submarines, airplanes, bombs, and missiles?"

The *New York Times* article was followed a few days after the Navy Seals' rescue by an editorial entitled "Fighting Piracy in Somalia" that concluded:

> Yet left to its own devices, Somalia can only become more noxious, spreading violence to its East African neighbors, breeding more extremism and making shipping through the Gulf of Aden ever more dangerous and costly. Various approaches are being discussed, such as working through Somalia's powerful clans to reconstitute first local and then regional and national institutions. These must be urgently explored.[2]

Nowhere did the *New York Times*—or any of the other media outlets that I read, heard, or saw—attempt to analyze the roots of the problem in Somalia. Debates abounded about whether to arm ships' crews and send more Navy vessels to the region. There was that vague reference to reconstituting regional and national institutions, but what exactly did the author mean by that? Institutions that would truly help, like free hospitals, schools, and soup kitchens? Or local militias, prisons, and Gestapo-style police forces?

The pirates were fishermen whose livelihoods had been destroyed. They were fathers whose children were hungry. Ending piracy would require helping them live sustainable, dignified lives. Could journalists not understand this? Had none of them visited the slums of Mogadishu?

Finally, NPR's *Morning Edition* on May 6 aired a report from Gwen Thompkins; she interviewed a pirate who went by the name Abshir Abdullahi Abdi.

"We understand what we're doing is wrong," Abdi explained. "But hunger is more important than any other thing."

Thompkins commented, "Fishing villages in the area have been devastated by illegal trawlers and waste dumping from industrialized nations. Coral reefs are reportedly dead. Lobster and tuna have vanished. Malnutrition is high."[3]

You might think we would have learned from Vietnam, Iraq, the "Black Hawk down" incident in Somalia back in 1993, and other such forays, that military responses seldom discourage insurgencies. In fact, they often do the opposite; foreign intervention is likely to infuriate local populations, motivate them to support the rebels, and result in an escalation of resistance activities. That was the way it happened during the American Revolution, Latin America's War for Independence from Spain, in colonial Africa, Indochina, Soviet-occupied Afghanistan, and so many other places.

Blaming pirates and other desperate people for our problems is a distraction we cannot afford if we truly want to find a solution to the crises confronting us. These incidents are symptoms of our failed economic model. They are to our society the equivalent of a heart attack to an individual. We send in Navy Seals to rescue the hostages, as we would hire doctors to perform a coronary artery bypass. But it is essential to admit that both are reactions to an underlying problem. The patient needs to address the reasons his or her heart failed in the first place, such as smoking, diet, and lack of exercise. The same is true for piracy and all forms of terrorism.

Our children's futures are interlocked with the futures of children born in the fishing villages of Somalia, the mountains of Burma (Myanmar), and the jungles of Colombia. When we forget that fact, when we see those children as remote, as somehow disconnected from our lives, as merely the offspring of pirates, guerrillas, or drug runners, we point the gun at our own progeny as well as at the desperate fathers and mothers in lands that seem so far away but in reality are our next-door neighbors.

Every time I read about the actions we take to protect ourselves from so-called terrorists, I have to wonder at the narrow-mindedness of our strategy. Although I have met such people in Bolivia, Ecuador, Egypt, Guatemala, Indonesia, Iran, and Nicaragua, I have never met one who wanted to take up a gun. I know there are crazed men and women who kill because they cannot stop themselves, serial killers, and mass-murderers. I am certain that members of Al Qaeda, the Taliban, and other such groups are driven by fanaticism, but such extremists are able to recruit sizable numbers of followers only from populations that feel oppressed or destitute. The "terrorists" I have found in Andean caves and desert villages are people whose families were forced off their farms by oil companies, hydroelectric dams, or "free trade" agreements. Their children are starving, and they want nothing more than to return to their families with food, seeds, and deeds to lands they can cultivate.

In Mexico, many of the guerillas and narcotraffickers once owned farms where they grew corn. They lost their livelihoods when the

North American Free Trade Agreement (NAFTA) gave subsidized U.S. producers an unfair price advantage. Here is how the Organic Consumers Organization, a nonprofit that represents more than 850,000 members, subscribers, and volunteers, describes it:

> Since NAFTA came into effect on January 1, 1994, U.S. corn exports to Mexico have almost doubled to some 6 million metric tons in 2002. NAFTA eliminated quotas limiting corn imports . . . but allowed U.S. subsidy programs to remain in place—promoting dumping of corn into Mexico by U.S. agribusiness at below the cost of production. . . . The price paid to farmers in Mexico for corn fell by over 70 percent. . . .[4]

The passage above exposes the dark side of "free trade" policies. U.S. presidents and our Congress have implemented regulations that prohibited other countries from imposing tariffs on U.S. goods or subsidizing locally grown produce that might compete with our agribusinesses while permitting us to maintain our own import barriers and subsidies, thus giving U.S. corporations an unfair advantage. "Free trade" is a euphemism; it prohibits others from enjoying the benefits offered to the multinationals. It does not, however, regulate against the pollution that is melting glaciers, the land grabs, and the sweatshops.

The Nicaraguan priest who had ministered to Sandinista guerrillas and was now president of the U.N. General Assembly has a firsthand appreciation for such euphemisms and the power of words used to sway public perceptions. "Terrorism is not really an 'ism,' " Father Miguel d'Escoto told me. "There's no connection between the Sandinistas who fought the Contras and Al Qaeda, or Colombia's FARC and fishermen turned pirates in Africa and Asia. Yet they are all called 'terrorists.' That's just a convenient way for your government to convince the world that there is another enemy 'ism' out there, like communism used to be. It diverts attention from the very real problems.'"

Our narrow-minded attitudes and the resultant policies foment violence, rebellions, and wars. In the long run, almost no one benefits from attacking the people we label as "terrorists." With one glaring exception: the corporatocracy.

Those who own and run the companies that build ships, missiles, and armored vehicles; make guns, uniforms, and bulletproof vests; distribute food, soft drinks, and ammunition; provide insurance, medicines, and toilet paper; construct ports, airstrips, and housing; and reconstruct devastated villages, factories, schools, and hospitals—they, and only they, are the big winners.

The rest of us are hoodwinked by that one, loaded word: *terrorist*.

The current economic collapse has awakened us to the importance of regulating and reining in the people who control the businesses that benefit from the misuse of words like *terrorism* and who perpetrate other scams. We recognize today that white-collared executives are not a special incorruptible breed. Like the rest of us, they require rules. Yet it is not enough for us to reestablish regulations that separate investment banks from commercial banks and insurance companies, reinstate anti-usury laws, and impose guidelines to ensure that consumers are not burdened by credit they cannot afford. We cannot simply return to solutions that worked before. Only by adopting new strategies that promote global environmental and social responsibility will we safeguard the future.

One of the world's great spiritual leaders, the Dalai Lama, clearly understands and promotes this. He expressed his version of a call for action one morning when I sat beside him on an airplane flying over the Himalayas.

CHAPTER 18

The Dalai Lama

Prayer AND Action!

Our group arrived very early at the airport in Leh, Ledakh. As we sat waiting for our flight to India to be announced, the Dalai Lama and his entourage swept into the tiny lobby. We had heard him speak to a crowd of thousands of Tibetans several days earlier but had been unable to arrange a private meeting with him.

One of our group excitedly told me that the Dalai Lama was carrying my book *Shapeshifting*. Someone else informed his secretary that the author of that book was on his flight. When we boarded, I was immediately ushered to the front of the Boeing 737.

The Dalai Lama smiled up at me and patted the seat beside him. "Wonderful," he said as he tapped the cover of *Shapeshifting*. "I'd like to learn more."

The plane took off. He pointed down at the Himalayas and named several of the Buddhist monasteries I had visited. Then he and I chatted about indigenous people and their commitments to living sustainable lives. I explained that the reason the Shuar in the Amazon go to war and shrink enemy heads is because one of their gods commanded that if their populations get out of control, "you must weed your own garden." That god was angry at the Shuar because their growing numbers were causing the extinction of other species—both plants and animals.

The Dalai Lama nodded and then was silent for a moment. When he spoke, he admitted that while he did not condone violence he could understand that god's point. "Peace is possible," he said, "only when we humans show compassion for all sentient beings. We must take responsibility for protecting life." He added that it was important that we *act* in responsible ways, not just think, talk, and pray about it.

I mentioned that a famous writer from the West had recently called on everyone to stop what they were doing on a specific day at a certain time and pray for peace.

"Prayer is very good," he responded, "like meditation. But not enough." He went on to express concern that if millions of people across the planet prayed for peace and then ended by feeling they had done their jobs, believing that the prayers were all that was necessary, we would probably never have peace. "We need to take action." He broke into that smile of his I had seen on the covers of his books. "Yes, we must act."

At the end of the flight, the Dalai Lama invited our group to his home in Dharmasala, India. A couple of days later, we spent the better part of an afternoon chatting with him there. It was a deeply moving and inspiring exchange that encompassed a wide range of topics. Yet the thing that impressed me most was his emphasis on taking action. Here was one of the world's great spiritual leaders stressing the importance not of prayer or meditation but of concrete action.

Later, when our group assembled back at the hotel, one of the women pointed out that Christ, Confucius, Mohammed, Buddha, Gandhi, Martin Luther King Jr., and Nelson Mandela had made similar statements.

"Action is essential," a neuroscientist friend told me after I returned home and related my discussion with the Dalai Lama to him. "But it's important to recognize that there are a couple of steps that precede the action. This is where the prayer that writer was promoting—for peace—comes into play, or the Dalai Lama's meditation, or what your indigenous friends might refer to as the 'dream.' " He pointed at a glass of water on the table between us. "Before I can pick up that glass, I have to be motivated."

"Thirst."

"Sure. Or maybe I want to clear the table." He grinned. "Or throw the water at you. It doesn't really matter; the thing is I have to be motivated. Then I have to believe I can do it. I have to 'dream' of doing it. My brain has to send signals to my arm and hand that I want, and am able, to pick up that glass." He peered at me. "There are hundreds of people relegated to mental institutions because their minds can't send out those kinds of signals." He bent forward and reached for the glass. "After I've done all that, then I can swing into action." He picked it up, raised it to his lips, and stopped. "Now [an impish smile] I have to decide. Do I drink? Or throw it at you?"

Collectively, we are staring at that glass. Decision time is here. What shall we do with it?

In the historic perspective of economic development, our species has progressed from infancy to adolescence. Metaphorically, as hunters and gatherers, we crawled on the earth. After a while we straightened, wielded the hoe, and became cultivators. Rather than accepting that we could receive only things that were offered by nature, we took steps to gain more control. We planted and harvested, studied weather patterns and crop cycles, domesticated animals, and learned to create fabrics and weave cloth. We hammered out tools—and weapons. Then, perhaps beginning with small nomadic bands sweeping down from the Asian Steppes into the more fertile regions of the Middle East and Europe, we plundered. We grew enamored with the possibilities of exploiting others. We became competitive and aggressive. We organized ourselves into societies whose goals were to outcompete their neighbors. We bought into the idea that resources are finite, that in order for "our" people to have more, we have to take from someone else.

Previous chapters of this book have followed our economic evolution from mercantilism to industrialization and to this time when competition is seen as revolving around finance, communications, and computer technologies and when nations have been replaced by multinational corporations as the driving forces behind geopolitics.

Now, in the face of the worldwide recession, we sense a frustration around our accomplishments. We confront the knowledge that we are self-destructing. The crises symbolized by melting glaciers are beginning to convince us that it is time to move beyond the old principles that have guided us through the past centuries, to push ourselves along the economic development curve—to abandon that exploitative, colonialist, adolescent attitude and embrace a mature recognition that we are a fragile species living on a very tiny planet.

The hour has arrived for us to understand that my grandson cannot live a satisfying life unless all his brothers and sisters around the world also live satisfying lives. Homeland security will become a reality only when we accept the entire planet as our homeland. It is time for us to act as though we are all in this together and our very existence depends on cooperation. Because both those things are true.

We have arrived at the point where we know we must insist that our business and political leaders guide us along the path to a future that leads to long-term sustainability, justice, and peace—for all people. We know too that it is up to us to insist that they do this. Our leaders must be pushed.

Past empires expanded through military conquests. This has

changed. The current forces controlling the world were not built by armies, but through corporations. We need to act, but we do not need to take up arms to transform them.

The next chapters present a strategy for implementing change that encompasses five arenas of action:

1. Accepting consumer responsibility

2. Creating a new economy

3. Adopting attitudes that encourage good stewardship and make icons of a new type of hero

4. Implementing new rules for business and government

5. Honoring our individual passions

If relatively few of us, a critical mass—a tiny percentage of the population—consciously takes action in each of these arenas, we will succeed. In our lifetime.

CHAPTER 19

Accepting Consumer Responsibility

"Refuse to purchase another Nike product," a woman at one of my talks said as she stood and waved her hands over the audience, "and send an e-mail to Nike explaining that you won't buy anything from them until they stop using sweatshops. Instead, buy from one of the 'sweat-free' companies—they are on the Internet—and send them an e-mail telling them it's because they don't use sweatshops. If enough of us do that, Nike will have to change—or go out of business."

"What happens to all the Indonesians who worked in those sweatshops?" a man across the room shouted.

I stepped to the microphone. "No one needs to lose a job," I said. "The goal is to convince companies like Nike that they must turn sweatshops into legitimate factories where the workers get wages that allow them to live decent lives, including the ability to pay for health care and retirement."

Another woman raised her hand. "Are you telling me," she asked, "that I have to spend more for my kids' shirts and tennis shoes so I can support some family in Asia? I already work two jobs and can hardly make ends meet."

I answered by relating a story about my daughter, Jessica. She called one day back when she was pregnant. She had been shopping for cribs online. "I found one," she said, "for $200. It's made in China, probably at a sweatshop. There's another that's manufactured in a nonsweatshop Canadian factory and constructed from woods that are certified not to come from old-growth or rain forest trees. It costs $600. What do you think, Dad?"

I looked out over the assembled people and told them that Jessica worked for a nonprofit organization; she did not make much money and was very careful about how she spent every penny.

"Of course, I'll pay the extra $400," she continued over the phone. "I'd somehow scrape together $400 for a car seat to protect my baby's life. Or a day care center that I know is safe. So why not do it to create a world that will be just and safe? It's an investment in his future, not a sacrifice."

I told that audience—as I have many others—that paying more for products made by companies that are socially and environmentally responsible is always an investment in the future. It means we are not passing that debt on to our children. "Sometimes," I say, "you may not be able to afford the investment. You may have to purchase the cheaper item. If that happens, at least be conscious that you're forgoing an investment. Beyond that, though, make a commitment to yourself that when you can afford it, you will do the smart thing, the thing that is best for you and your children over the long term."

As consumers, we have tremendous power. This book has emphasized that the marketplace is a democratic voting booth. We the people can decide to use our purchasing leverage to encourage good stewardship.

When we stopped purchasing gas-guzzling SUVs, during periods of escalating oil prices, auto manufacturers closed factories.

The same thing occurred with children's toys from China after we learned they contained carcinogens, with cigarettes following campaigns that exposed the health problems they posed to children who breathed secondary smoke, with asbestos in building materials, and with many other products.

Some management theorists speculate that one reason CEOs of big corporations are paid so much money is that they are among a rare few who have the proper skills and that they also lack the type of consciences that prohibit most of us from selling products and making decisions that destroy lives. Thom Hartmann writes,

> [O]nly about 1 to 3 percent of us are sociopaths, . . . and of that 1 percent, there's probably only a fraction of a percent with a college education, . . . an even tinier fraction that understands how business works. . . . Thus there is such a shortage of people who can run modern monopolistic, destructive corporations that stockholders have to pay millions of dollars to get them to work. And being sociopaths, they gladly take the money without any thought of its social consequences.[1]

Perhaps sociopaths do indeed sit at the top of some of our largest corporations—but that should not deter us. They depend on us to buy their goods and services. They do not command militaries that force us to purchase their products.

Most of the executives I know—including ones I met during my EHM years—are not sociopaths. Rather, they are infected by this same mutant form of capitalism. They are driven by the belief that their job is to make profits. Period. When offered the opportunity, they hurry to attend corporate social responsibility (CSR) conferences. They embrace the idea of the triple bottom line. Once we empower them to consider goals other than profit, they act with enthusiasm.

A Portland, Oregon, radio host recently asked me, "If you could give one piece of advice to Phil Knight [Nike founder and chairman of the board], what would it be?"

"I'd suggest," I answered, "that he follow Henry Ford's example. Ford said he wanted to pay his workers enough so they could buy a Ford. If Nike did the same wherever it has sweatshops, this would be a much safer and better world. And Nike's sales would skyrocket."

On the air we discussed the fact that Nike has taken steps to become more environmentally responsible and has invested a great deal of money into public relations efforts to convince us that its workers are better off today than they were a few years ago. However, Jim Keady and Leslie Kretzu, the cofounders of Educating for Justice described in Chapter 4, along with other NGOs that monitor the situation in Indonesia and elsewhere, have found that the people who produce Nike products in many of these countries are still terribly underpaid and work in abysmal conditions.

I do not know Phil Knight or his psychological profile. It is possible that he is one of those sociopaths. If so, he is not likely to subscribe to Ford's philosophy. However, we the consumers—you and I—can force him to treat his workers humanely. We simply stop buying Nike products until the company changes its policies.

I told that radio audience in Portland, "I would like nothing better than to wear the Nike swoosh as a symbol of a company that is doing everything possible to make this a better world. That time will come if we all refuse to wear the swoosh until Nike makes a commitment to take care of the people who produce its products."

Two other questions are regularly asked during the Q&A periods after my talks:

1. What about corporations that supply the military: How do we turn them around?

2. How can I judge a corporation's commitment to behaving in socially and environmentally responsible ways?

The short answer to the first question is that we have more influence over the military-oriented businesses than we may think. Organizations like Rainforest Action Network (RAN) have found that corporations that are not retailers—like Boise Cascade and most military suppliers—or ones that are in businesses where they do not believe the consumer develops any particular product loyalty—like Citigroup and military suppliers—have their own sets of leverage points.

"You request the help of their biggest buyers," Mike Brune, RAN's executive director told me one day as we sat in a San Francisco restaurant. "When Boise Cascade refused to negotiate, we enlisted Kinko's and some of Boise's other customers who had already signed on to our program. The pressure worked. With the big banks, you may have to embarrass their top executives." RAN has published photos of corporate presidents in newspaper ads with captions about destroying forests and murdering indigenous people, and it has dispatched members armed with placards and banners to speeches given by corporate officials—an approach similar to that used by the women's suffrage movement against Woodrow Wilson. Both approaches brought results. "Corporate executives," Mike continued, "are people; they have to face their children. They respond to social pressures just like you and me."

A longer answer to this question about influencing the military-industrial complex has to do with changing the economy. It is addressed in the next chapters.

The second question often asked is about assessing a corporation's commitment.

As Jessica found when looking for my grandson's crib, a great deal of information is available over the Internet. While sources are not always accurate, they are constantly updated, and improvements are made on an almost daily basis. Google and other search engines are good resources for making sure that we obtain the most current data. At the time of this writing, one helpful source was the website of the nonprofit Green America (formerly Co-op America). For example, based upon their research, if you wanted to know about tennis shoes, here's what Co-Op America said in April 2009:

SNEAKERS: LEADERS AND LAGGARDS

Footwear can be one of the trickiest parts of building a sweatshop-free wardrobe. Hundreds of shoe companies have shifted their operations overseas in recent years, and many have little or no oversight for their supply chains.

We used two of Co-op America's online tools (ResponsibleShopper.org and GreenPages.org) to build this list of "leaders and laggards" in the athletic-shoe industry. Click the links on the company names below to learn more about the conventional companies at Responsible Shopper, or to find the green businesses' listings in the *Green Pages*.

The Autonomie Project: Produces sneakers made with Forest Stewardship Council certified all-natural and sustainable latex sole. The company pays Fair Trade premiums to both the rubber producers in Sri Lanka and to the shoe stitchers in Pakistan. *Grade: A+*

Equita: Sells sneakers from the Paris-based Veja company. Veja works directly with Brazilian cooperatives to source eco-friendly organic cotton and natural latex for its sneakers, which are made under fair labor conditions, including living wages and long-term relationships with producers. *Grade: A+*

Global Exchange: Offers No Sweat sneakers in its online Fair Trade store. *Grade: A+*

No Sweat Apparel: Produces sneakers at a unionized factory in Indonesia. Wage and benefit information for the workers appears on No Sweat's website, including maternity benefits, Ramadan bonuses, health insurance coverage, and more. *Grade: A+*

Traditions Fair Trade: Sells sneakers made by Argentinean cooperatives. Traditions' website links to The Working World, a nonprofit entity that supports the cooperatives, where shoppers can view a breakdown of where each penny of the purchase price of the shoes is going. *Grade: A+*

New Balance: As a conventional shoe company, New Balance is unique in making more than one quarter of its products in the United States. Its shift toward Chinese manufacturing in recent years has opened the company to criticisms, such as the low wages and long hours documented in a 2006 report by National Labor Committee (NLC) and China Labor Watch. *Grade: C*

Timberland: Timberland utilizes a third-party assessment system for independent monitoring of its manufacturing facilities, but the factories from which Timberland sources have still been cited for unfair overtime, unsanitary conditions, and late pay. *Grade: C*

Nike: Recent factory-level abuses have included the firings of worker-organizers at one of Nike's Turkish factories to prevent union activity. *Grade: F*

Reebok/Adidas: Recent labor abuses at Reebok's Jordanian factories include human trafficking of guest workers, confiscation of passports, sixteen-hour shifts, wages below the legal minimum, beatings, and sexual assault. *Grade: F*

Puma: Repeatedly implicated in egregious violations of

workers' rights in Turkey, China, El Salvador, Indonesia, and
Mexico. Reports from Bangladesh included child workers
being beaten, suffering from exhaustion, working manda-
tory fourteen-hour days, and paid as little as 6½ cents an
hour. *Grade: F* [2]

If you desired more information on a specific company, you
could have gone to another page on that same website. For Nike
you would have learned the following:

- Nike is the number 1 shoe company in the world and controls over one-fifth of the athletic shoe market in the United
  States.

- Nike discloses its factory locations and employs independent
  monitors to assess compliance with the company's supplier
  code of conduct, and for purchasing a majority of its energy
  needs from green sources.

- However, Nike critics maintain that these efforts do not go
  far enough to improve conditions for garment workers.

- There have been accusations of repeated labor violations at
  Nike supplier plants where employees are underpaid, over-
  worked, and commonly face verbal and even physical abuse.

- Nike allegedly lied about conditions at overseas factories
  where their shoes and clothes are manufactured, in an
  attempt to guard the company from criticism for human
  rights and labor violations, and as a result the California
  Supreme Court ruled that Nike can be sued for false advertising after it was found that the company's statements
  in defense of overseas labor conditions were "commercial
  speech."[3]

New tools are evolving all the time to make it easier for consumers to use the marketplace as a polling booth. Even as truth-in-labeling practices have revolutionized our ability to analyze foods—to know how many calories and how much fat, protein, fiber, sodium, vitamins and other ingredients they contain—in the near future we will be better able to determine the social and environmental conditions under which our clothes, appliances, and other products are made.

Daniel Goleman discusses "Social and Environmental Life Cycle Analysis (SELCA) bar code labeling" in his new book *Ecological Intelligence* as an approach that is just around the corner. It is a process that will include a bar code on every product that can be read at the point of purchase by a small camera imbedded in personal cell phones. All the good and bad aspects of a product will be taken into account, including those at the beginning of its life cycle such as the mining or farming operations and those at the end—that is, the costs and benefits of disposal and/or recycling.[4]

Such evolving techniques will allow us to hone our skills. Yet, we must not wait. Sufficient information is available now for us to make an impact. We cannot expect 100 percent perfection from ourselves or the corporations—at least not at the beginning—but we can expect a 100 percent commitment from all of us to strive for perfection. It is our privilege, and duty, to send out the word that we will patronize only those companies that are dedicated to providing goods and services that embrace the strictest principles of environmental and social responsibility.

The process of reaching toward perfection offers limitless opportunities. It opens doors for a new generation of enterprising inventors, entrepreneurs, and business executives. Eliminating the mutant virus allows us to explore new forms of healthy capitalism, to step into an exciting and dynamic economy. That is the subject of the next chapter.

CHAPTER 20

Creating a New Economy

"The big agribusiness companies used a lot of fertilizers, insecticides, and other chemicals," Nicaragua's minister of agriculture and forestry, Ariel Bucardo Rocha, said, looking at Stephan Rechtschaffen. "Much of our land has been destroyed."

Stephan, an MD by training, had cofounded the Omega Institute in 1977 as an educational center dedicated to personal growth, health, and transformation. He is also author of the book *Time Shifting*. Now he was building a new holistic learning center in Costa Rica and exploring ways to promote organic farming throughout the region. He had organized this trip to Nicaragua in March 2008 for a small group of philanthropists and social activists who were interested in helping Nicaraguan *campesinos*. We had traveled to remote locations, talked with farmers, visited local markets, and returned to Managua where we were meeting with government officials.

We kept hearing the same story. Companies like Dole, Chiquita, Cargill, and Kraft had ravaged the land. Policies that were aimed solely at maximizing corporate profits had rendered the soil so infertile that organic farming was now impossible in many parts of the country.

The impacts of some of these methods are summarized in a *SourceWatch* article:

Chiquita workers in Nicaragua, Costa Rica, Honduras, and elsewhere have accused the company of using toxic agro-chemicals, including pesticides outlawed in other countries including the U.S., in the production of their bananas. In 2002, a Nicaraguan court sentenced Chiquita, Dole, and Dow to pay $489 million in damages to Nicaraguan workers suffering from injuries incurred from contact with the pesticide Nemagon, also known as DBCP, which was banned in the U.S. decades before, after it was proven to cause severe health effects, including vision loss, organ damage, infertility, cancer, birth defects, and miscarriages.[1]

"It's hard to believe that foreign companies would push chemicals that are illegal in the United States—because they are so dangerous—off onto another country," Alba Palacios, a member of the Directing Council of Nicaragua's General Assembly, told us. "But that's exactly what happened here."

Besides farmlands, Nicaragua also is endowed with an abundance of fresh water. Its many rivers and small lakes are complemented by two huge lakes: Lake Nicaragua, with an area of more than 3,000 square miles, the largest lake in Central America; and Lake Managua, approximately forty miles long and fifteen miles wide. Unfortunately the nation's water is terribly polluted. The U.S. nonprofit Public Citizen reported:

Although water covers 10 percent of Nicaragua's surface, environmental degradation, pollution, and simple scarcity in some regions threaten the country's ability to provide enough water to sustain its population and productivity. Today, near a third of Nicaraguans do not have access to potable water. In rural areas, where 72 percent of people lack such access, people must often procure their water

from shallow wells, rivers, streams, and lakes that are polluted with residential sewage, pesticides, and industrial
toxins.²

Stephan and I stood together on the shore of Lake Managua the
day after our meetings with Mses. Rocha and Palacios. The stench
was almost unbearable. "After the 1972 earthquake, Somoza took
all that foreign aid money," Stephan mused, referring to Anastasio
("Tachito") Somoza Debayle, who ruled Nicaragua, often brutally,
from 1967 to 1979 and whose family had run the country with an
iron hand since 1936. "He lived like a king. Instead of rebuilding
Managua and its water and sewer systems, he siphoned all the
human, industrial, and agricultural wastes into this lake. He turned
it into a cesspool."

"That was during my second year as an EHM." I raised a ban-
dana to my nose as protection against the noxious fumes. "I re-
call that those earthquake funds were earmarked to stimulate an
economic miracle along this shoreline—beautiful homes, parks, a
boardwalk, shops, art galleries, perhaps an open air theater. Tour-
ism and increasing real estate values would allow Nicaragua to pay
off its debts and continue to prosper."

"Instead, this whole shoreline is uninhabitable. What a lost
opportunity!"

I told Stephan about a dinner I attended not long after the
earthquake. World Bank president Robert McNamara was the
speaker. Afterward, a small group of us who were involved in Latin
American projects met with McNamara. He let us know that the
bank and the U.S. government (McNamara had been secretary of
defense under JFK and LBJ) would stand behind Somoza, despite
the corruption and human rights abuses, because he was "a bas-
tion against Communists like Castro and Torrijos." The words had
shocked me. I wondered at the time how a man with McNamara's

education could denigrate Omar Torrijos as a Communist, but I held my tongue—and kept my job.

Stephan and I then discussed the possibilities of reforming the World Bank. "Its original mission was a good one," I said. "To reconstruct countries devastated by World War II. Seems like now's the time to bring that mission to places like this." We discussed the idea that the United Nations could work with the World Bank, directing a major campaign to clean up the lake and convert a wasteland next to Nicaragua's capital city into a model for urban planning.

"Imagine," Stephan said, "what could happen if a portion of the United States' military budget paid some of the companies that currently manufacture missiles and tanks to instead make equipment that could clean up this lake."

It is an intriguing concept and one that could also be applied to other industries. For example, what might happen if some of our tax dollars paid Dole, Chiquita, Cargill, Kraft, and other agribusinesses to develop ways in which the starving people of the world could feed themselves—better methods for growing, storing, and distributing food locally. No need to put anyone out of work. Just change their jobs. Instead of submarines, pay the creative minds at General Dynamics, Raytheon, and Grumman to make boats that clean up polluted lakes. Instead of banana plantations, hire Chiquita, Dole, and Kraft to develop facilities that refurbish depleted soils and develop food storage systems tailored to poor rural communities.

"You stroll through Wal-Mart and you realize," Stephan said, "that the world is full of junk no one needs. Walk down the aisles of a supermarket and you're struck by the variety of decisions we all have to make. Corn flakes—with or without sugar? Or honey? Raisins added or not? Maybe dehydrated strawberries? Brand X or Y? Large yellow box or even larger family-size orange box?"

"Meanwhile a billion or more people are on the verge of starving."

We strolled along a stretch of crumbling concrete where years before someone had begun building a walkway-by-the water or something else I could not identify. It now lay in ruins. I kept thinking about how so much of our global economy today is based on junk, items that serve no useful purpose. All the plastics and metals that are wasted. The grains that are processed into foods that offer no nutrition and are wrapped in fancy wasteful packages. The cell phones, laptop computers, and other electronic gadgets that turn obsolete within months and have as a key component the rare mineral known as coltan that is mined by starving Africans. And I kept visualizing the faces and emaciated bodies of hungry people—the ones I had met in India, Nepal, Indonesia, and Haiti and the ones I, like everyone else, had seen on TV. I tried not to be depressed, to instead contemplate the possibilities of a new economy based on producing things that people actually need, and goods and services that serve the earth and offer hope for the future.

I mentioned to Stephan my belief that a revolution is sweeping through the hemisphere. Nicaragua is one of ten countries in Latin America that have voted in a new wave of presidents, each one democratically elected. These countries—representing more than 80 percent of the population of South America—in the last few years have elected presidents who sent the world a resounding message. They said "no" to the colonialist policies that have relegated their people to servitude for centuries. They said "no" to the predatory form of capitalism that they usually refer to as the "Washington Consensus," "neocolonialism," or "neoliberalism." They demanded the demolition of the walls that had imprisoned them in World Bank and IMF debts. They served notice that they will no longer tolerate the plundering of resources and the privatization of the public sector by multinational corporations.

Every one of these countries—Argentina, Bolivia, Brazil, Chile, Ecuador, Nicaragua, Paraguay, El Salvador, Uruguay, and Venezuela—during much of my lifetime was ruled by repressive governments and brutal dictators, often with CIA support. These unelected officials had helped the corporatocracy rape their nations' resources. Now, in less than a decade, all that has changed. The people have spoken. Peacefully, in democratic elections, they have voted in presidents who understand that the key to transformation lies in recognizing the value of their resources and their citizens' rights to benefit from those resources—as well as their responsibilities to use them in ways that will help future generations. Significantly, these leaders also comprehend the power of corporations; they know that in order for their people to realize their objectives, they must encourage—or force—corporations to change their most basic goal.

These new Latin American leaders have opened the door to a new economy. In opening that door, they are showing the rest of us a way to combine a form of capitalism that produces things the world truly needs with the goal of making profits while creating a sustainable, just, and peaceful world.

A breeze came up and blew off Lake Managua. The stench from the polluted waters was now unbearable. Stephan and I turned away and headed back to our parked car. Walking across the pockmarked concrete, we lamented the terrible environmental destruction that has occurred in our lifetimes.

I kept reflecting, as we drove down the streets of Managua toward our hotel, on the idea that what we really need to do is move beyond the extreme materialism and militarism that characterize our current economy. It struck me that there were already some pretty good models out there of what the new economy might look like. One of those was high in the Andes. Others were right in our own backyard, in places like Chicago, Denver, San Francisco, Seattle, and Washington, D.C.

CHAPTER 21

Green Markets

Otavalo is a postcard-perfect town perched high in the Ecuadorian Andes. At an altitude of over 8,000 feet, it is located just a few miles north of the equator and is nestled in a valley formed by three volcanoes considered sacred by local populations. It is home to an indigenous tribe that shares its name, traces its origins back to long before the Incas, and is famous for its musicians, weavers, and shamans.

Jorge Tamayo was one of those shamans and also my *compadre*, the father of my godson. We strolled together through the market one sunny morning. The thin Andean air smelled of wood smoke. The melancholic music of pan pipes, flutes, and drums played by a local band competed for our attention with the shouts of weavers hawking sweaters, shawls, ponchos, and tapestries that hung from their stalls and from lines strung between them in such a brilliant profusion of color that we could have been passing through a rainbow.

"Wool from our own sheep and llamas," Jorge explained. "Everything made in the homes of our families." He stopped to chat with an old woman. Her clothes were the traditional straight dark blue skirt that reached to sandals woven from the fibers of the agave plant, a white blouse with red and green embroidered flowers, and a necklace of gold beads wrapped several times around her throat. "Did you make this yourself, grandmother?" he asked picking up a red-trimmed blue poncho and offering it for my inspection.

Her creased face broke into a smile that flashed gold teeth. "My daughter did," she said proudly. "These days, my eyes aren't so good. I do most of the selling. My children and grandchildren tend the animals and are the weavers."

It was the poncho I had been searching for as a gift for a friend. Jorge bargained with the lady, I bought it, and we walked on. "I often think of this market," he said, "when I go to your country." He had a U.S. visa, and he traveled to New England where his talents as a shaman and his knowledge of Andean traditions were in demand. "Everyone there talks about the environment and tells me not to buy certain products because they're made by people who are mistreated." He stopped and looked about. "Here we don't have to worry about that."

I told him I felt the same. Since my first visit to Otavalo's market in 1969, I had been impressed with both the quality of the work and the fact it was all done by local people using local materials. In recent years, though, things had begun to change. Now some stalls sold items imported from Peru and even Asia. At the same time, however, change was coming to my country; it seemed that the pendulum had begun to swing in the other direction.

"On your next visit to the States," I said, "I'll take you to markets that are similar to this one—not in the products they sell or the way they look, but philosophically." I was thinking of the Green Festivals held each year in Chicago, Denver, San Francisco, Seattle, and Washington, D.C.

A joint project of Global Exchange and Green America, the Green Festivals feature more than 350 ecofriendly businesses—everything from organic body care lotions, tennis shoes, and clothes to fair trade foods and home and garden products made from renewable resources. All Green Festival exhibitors are screened for their commitment to sustainable business practices. More than 25,000 people typically walk through the marketplace in any given city. Besides the stalls, there are other activities, including speeches by business leaders, authors, and educators; workshops; films; activities for children; organic beer, wine, and cuisine; and live music.

One of the speakers at a recent festival was Thom Hartmann, author of *The Last Hours of Ancient Sunlight, What Would Jefferson Do, Threshold,* and more than a dozen other books, and host of an Air America radio show. During his talk he pointed out something that particularly struck me and also is stated in *Threshold*:

> At a certain level, our modern consumer society is built on a truth and a lie. The truth is that if you're living below the threshold of safety and security, a little bit of "stuff" can create a huge change in your mental and emotional states and the quality of your life. . . .
>
> The lie is the siren song of our culture. "If that much stuff will generate that much instant happiness," the lie goes, "then ten times as much stuff will make you ten times happier. . . ."[1]

It seemed a fitting observation in the context of those two types of markets—the first located in one of the hemisphere's poorest countries and the second in affluent, highly materialistic U.S. cities.

■ ■ ■

When I finish giving my speech at a Green Festival, I am hustled off to the bookstore within the marketplace. I sit there at a long table with several other authors and sign books. It is a wonderful opportunity to chat with people. They ask questions and sometimes pour their hearts out to me. Their words often reflect those of Thom Hartmann. We must learn, they say, that we in the States can live on much less, and yet there are people all over this globe who need so much more. The starving, desperate people have to receive a fairer share.

Afterward, I wander through the marketplace. As I examine the foods, clothes, shoes, and appliances, I am always impressed by the ingenuity of our people. There can be no doubt that the Green Festivals and other fairs and markets across the land are creating a new economy; we are on the verge of crafting a global marketplace with far-reaching implications.

I am also reminded that we the people did this—people like Denise Hamler, Alisa Gravitz, and Paul Freundlich who started Green America (formerly Co-op America); Kevin Danaher, Medea Benjamin, and Kirsten Moller who founded Global Exchange; and the thousands of men and women who are organizing green markets in towns and cities across the globe. A new type of thinking and inventiveness is infiltrating the world. It is apparent in the trees planted along Shanghai's highways and in China's commitment to replacing gas-guzzling cars with electric ones. It is apparent in the Port of Los Angeles's purchase of electric trucks capable of pulling 60,000-pound shipping containers that were developed by the innovative Balqon Corporation.[2] It is apparent in the Grameen Shakti Corporation's drive to turn Bangladesh into the world's first solar-driven economy, and in the array of goods TerraCycle produces from cookie and candy wrappers, potato chip bags, drink pouches, and other "wastes." It is apparent in the fancy purses and shoes made by Jade Planet from discarded plastic bags and in so many other goods and services that are entering our economy at accelerating rates.

A student from the University of Washington recently reminded me that when the car was popularized, the streets of our cities were inundated in horse manure and the farmers around those cities were struggling desperately to keep up with the daunting task of feeding the horses. "The automobile was hailed as our savior from pollution and food shortages," he said. "No solution is forever!"

Another student confessed that she would have to work for several years at some big corporation in order to pay off her student loans. "But then," she added with a glowing smile, "I'm going to build a company that will profit from cleaning up the floating island of garbage I sailed through in the Pacific Ocean two years ago."

In the last couple of months I have heard voices like those expressing similar thoughts in Ecuador, Iceland, Panama, and China. And across the United States. Last year I heard them in a number of other countries. They are the voices of our future, spoken by the people who are navigating our economy away from predatory capitalism into a vibrant new form.

The new economy will divert monies from manufacturing weapons to creating goods and services that bring harmony to our planet. It will transfer capital from developing chemical fertilizers, insecticides, and genetically modified organisms (GMOs) to implementing systems that facilitate local, organic farming techniques and empower starving people to feed themselves. It will reward companies that clean up the lakes of Nicaragua, replant the devastated forests of Borneo, and develop new technologies for harnessing renewable energy. It will remove needless items from our shelves—the trinkets and gadgets that serve no purpose except to make a few rich CEOs richer—and replace them with things that enhance life. This new economy will transport us from the adolescent attitudes that encourage us to exploit others into the mature recognition that we are one community living on a fragile planet. It will result in a more efficient distribution of goods and services and at the same time obliterate the terrible suffering that is at the root of most of this world's violence.

The people driving this new economy are today's entrepreneurs. They will prosper. They are the good stewards who will be tomorrow's heroes.

CHAPTER 22

Good Stewardship, New Icons

As a young man growing up in New Hampshire, my heroes, like those of everyone I knew, were people whose accomplishments made the world a better place for future generations. My friends and I wanted to follow in the footsteps of George Washington, Thomas Jefferson, Tom Paine, Harriet Tubman, Thomas Edison, Ralph Waldo Emerson, Harriet Beecher Stowe, Florence Nightingale, Elizabeth Cady Stanton, Susan B. Anthony, and (among soldiers) Dwight D. Eisenhower. We honored them not because they lived in big houses or accumulated wealth but because they were dedicated to noble causes.

In history classes, we were taught that although men like John D. Rockefeller and J. P. Morgan paved the way for industrialization, they were not the sort of people we wanted to emulate. They were portrayed as greedy, mean-spirited, and selfish.

Professor Ashton and his business school colleagues substantiated these beliefs in the late 1960s when they taught that corporate executives are fiduciary stewards charged with safeguarding long-term corporate interests. The laws enacted after the Great Depression codified this concept. Had the country continued honoring such beliefs in recent decades, we would not be suffering from today's economic calamity. Unfortunately, powerful people and interest groups pushed us in the opposite direction. And we went willingly.

We made icons of the likes of Donald Trump, a ruthless real estate developer who publicly glorifies the firing and humiliation of people on TV, and Jack Welch, the former chairman and CEO of GE who bragged about laying off one quarter of his company's employees while paying himself multi-million-dollar salaries and bonuses and denying that CO_2-polluting industries were seriously impacting the environment. We plaster the faces of billionaires on the covers of our magazines and praise them for donating fortunes to charity without bothering to point out that they made many times those fortunes by beating down their competitors. We watch shows about the rich and famous and in so doing, send messages to our children that they should aspire to living in mansions and traveling in private jets—regardless of how much environmental and social havoc is caused in the process. We display bumper stickers on our cars proclaiming "He who dies with the most toys wins."

During the past four decades, we the people have sent a strong message of support to the modern equivalent of the robber barons. We have let the executives know that we want them to provide us with inexpensive goods and high rates of return on our stocks. We have rewarded those CEOs who maximized profits, regardless of the cost.

Is that what we really want?

There is every indication that it is not. At least not any longer. The 2008 presidential election was symbolic in this regard. A major reason John McCain received the Republican nomination was because he had been viewed for years as a "maverick" and a decent, honest, selfless man who had chosen to remain a North Vietnamese prisoner of war rather than be released before his comrades because his father was a U.S. Navy admiral. When, during the campaign, people tried to entice McCain to proclaim that an Obama victory would cripple the country, he refused to do that. Obama ultimately won in large part because his platform presented a different, more magnanimous perspective than that offered by the Republicans.

In recent years we have witnessed many encouraging trends. Consumers are now sending messages that refute the old ones. We are saying that we want our leaders to look beyond profits, to provide goods and services that foster a better world. Many businesses are responding accordingly.

Companies like Whole Foods and Publix's Greenwise stores have proven that selling organically grown foods can be profitable. Novo Nordisk A/S, a Danish pharmaceutical company, is mission oriented toward ridding the world of diabetes. GrupoNueva of Chile has a goal of creating a sustainable Latin America. Grameen Danone Foods, a 50/50 joint venture between Groupe Danone—the $16 billion multinational yogurt maker—and the Grameen Group—an offshoot of the Grameen (microcredit) Bank founded by Nobel Peace laureate Muhammad Yunus—provides affordable nutrition to malnourished children in Bangladesh, as well as employment for their parents. Google.org has led the way into "for-profit philanthropy." Member-owned cooperatives have recently become a planet-encompassing business with more than 800 million members, double the number in the 1980s.

We are poised to enter a new era. Growing numbers of us recognize that it is time to stop honoring people who perpetuate a greedy, materialistic mentality, to cease buying magazines that feature their faces on the covers, and to switch off TV programs that try to convince us that squandering resources is something to be admired.

It is time to turn the Fortune 500 into a list of those corporations and NGOs that best serve the planet and future generations.

In 2005 when I dined with MBA students before my speeches at their schools and asked them to describe their goals, nearly all of them talked about making money and attaining power. In the fall of 2008 and the first half of 2009, I did not hear one student speak like this—not one MBA student from Stanford, Columbia, Wharton, the University of Michigan, Ohio State, Boston University, Harvard, Antioch, or the China Europe International Business School. Nor did I hear it from undergraduate students at Olivet College, Regis University, St. John's University, William Patterson University, or Wilmington College. Attitudes had changed in just three years. Not a single student who attended those dinners and other meetings with me listed as his or her goal the accumulation of either wealth or power. What they said instead was that they wanted to help create a better world.

Many of them wondered aloud why we do not demand more prime time television shows about the men and women who have founded and run our nonprofits. They suggested that such programs could include adventures in exotic locations, office intrigues, romance, sex, and eccentric characters who would be a whole lot more fun to watch than Donald Trump. Several students pointed out that the recent flurry of shows like *American Idol* are popular precisely because they glorify previously unknown people who have talent—in a way they are throwbacks to Ted Mack's *Original Amateur Hour* and Arthur Godfrey's *Talent Scouts* that gained popularity in the 1940s and 1950s, times when we seemed to place more value on ordinary people. A lot of students told me they were considering joining the Peace Corps or AmeriCorps, or planning on spending a year or two volunteering at nonprofit organizations.

A country's values may well be reflected in the images of its idols. That would explain the popularity, after World War II, of cowboy heroes who protected the defenseless against gunslingers and rancher barons. It would explain our obsession with wealth during a period when the leading economic theorist defined the sole objective of business as the maximization of profits. The corollary may also be true: The heroes we choose guide our young people into making decisions about how they will lead their lives. If we assume that either or both of these is the case, we can understand the importance at this point in history of honoring men and women who stand for a compassionate world view.

It is significant that two of the presidents leading Latin America into this new epoch are women (in Argentina and Chile), that many of the male presidents have committed to including a large percentage of women in their governments, and that during the 2008 U.S. presidential elections Hillary Clinton was runner-up for the Democratic nomination and Sarah Palin was the Republicans' vice presidential candidate. Statistics show, in most cases, that when women gain positions of power, greater emphasis is placed on the nurturing aspects of society and less on the militaristic ones. Police and defense budgets decrease and so do violence and crime rates.

In *Women, Power, and the Biology of Peace,* Dr. Judith Hand points out that men often see war as an opportunity to spread their sperm—one of their biological imperatives; on the other hand, for women war is a threat to the home, stability, and child raising. Women want peace and stability. Dr. Hand contends that in order for us to enjoy more peaceful societies, women must play larger roles in the decision-making processes.

Dr. Riane Eisler's book *The Real Wealth of Nations* concludes that in societies where women are respected as leaders and women make up a larger percentage of the government, such as in some of the northern European countries, more funding is allocated to health care, high-quality child care, education, and generously paid parental leaves. She states, "When the status and power of women is higher, so also is a nation's quality of life, and when it is lower, so is the quality of life for all."[1]

Abandoning our preoccupation with material wealth and profits and elevating ourselves to a more empathetic worldview will

require embracing feminine characteristics that foster peaceful communities and sustainable economies. More of our cultural icons in
the future will be women and also men who reflect the nurturing
aspects of leadership.

It is up to us to reverse the process that sprang out of the mutant
virus of capitalism that infected our economy. It is up to us to encourage an acceleration of the recent trends, to let our leaders know
that what we truly want is wholesome food, clean water and air, ac-
cessible health care, the assurance that we will be provided for after
retirement, legal systems that protect us and our rights—in short a
peaceful, just, and sustainable world. We want this for ourselves,
our children, and for every person on our planet. The hour has come
for us to honor and reward those men and women who strive to
achieve these goals.

Such leaders will understand the need to reinstate rules that
protect against the abuses that resulted in the current economic crises. They will also recognize the necessity of going beyond this and
instituting for the first time in history regulations that establish as
priorities a sustainable environment and a just and peaceful world
for the future.

CHAPTER 23

New Rules for Business and Government

Two Shuar men—Shakaim and Twitsa—and I hiked into the Cutucu mountains. We struggled up muddy slopes, forded shoulder-deep rivers, and hacked our way through the massive branches of a gigantic kapok tree that had fallen across the trail.

Finally we stood below the Sacred Waterfall. As it cascaded out of the mists, it created a rainbow that, according to a Shuar legend, birthed the first man and woman. Late in the afternoon, my companions taught me a traditional ceremony for honoring the water. That night, wrapped in blankets beneath a makeshift lean-to, we listened quietly to the growls of a passing jaguar.

The next afternoon, on our way back, only an hour away from their community, Shakaim raised his arm, signaling for us to stop. He and Twitsa stepped off the trail. They squatted beside a small plant, examined it, and exchanged words.

Shakaim cupped his hands around the plant and blew gently into it. Twitsa looked up at me. "It's sick," he explained, pointing at the leaves.

"It was healthy yesterday," Shakaim added, "when we came along this trail." He stood up. "We have to report this to the elders."

They resumed walking; I stood there gawking at that plant. I could see nothing exceptional about it, no reason why these men would have noticed it in the first place. A couple of leaves had turned brown and fallen to the ground, but that did not seem sufficient cause for concern.

That night, I received an education.

Shakaim, Twitsa, and their families gathered around a fire with other members of the community. They described in detail the state of the plant on the morning when we headed up to the waterfall and the changes that had occurred during the ensuing thirty-six hours. Their accounts were followed by lengthy discussions. The circle of participants paid particularly close attention to an old lady who was highly respected for her ability to prepare healing herbs. She suggested that the plant had delivered a message: The trail was overused.

A vote was taken. Although several people pointed out that there could have been other causes for the sickness, the decision was unanimous. If there was any possibility that people were contributing to the problem, then people had to take remedial action. A new rule was adopted for the entire community. That trail would be closed.

Outside the ceremonial lodge, Shakaim and I stood in the clearing and peered up at the starry night. "Interesting how different our regulations are from yours," he said as though hearing my question before I had a chance to verbalize it. "The priests make rules about who can have sex. The school has a law that children have to wear shoes." He paused. "But they don't say anything about not killing birds during mating season or abandoning trails when plants get sick." He pointed into the heavens. "How long do you think those stars would exist if the god who put them there was as shortsighted as the priests and schools?"

I thought of that experience a month later when I was back in the States where the idea of imposing greenhouse gas emissions limits on corporations was being debated by politicians and the media. The opposition argued that there was no absolute proof that CO_2 caused climate change. The contrast between the way the Shuar and the leaders of my country dealt with the world was striking. The "primitive" rain forest tribe did not require 100 percent certainty. It neither equivocated nor allowed short-term inconveniences to get in the way. If current actions might possibly threaten future generations, they regulated against them.

As populations and economies grow, one might expect the laws governing our relationship to the environment and society to become more stringent. Faced with greater demands for resources, it makes sense to charge some international governing body with the task of ensuring that they are allocated wisely. From a rational standpoint, protecting against the wanton destruction and depletion of things essential to our lives deserves the highest priority. However, the exact opposite has happened.

Recent scandals, beginning with Enron and continuing to Bernard Madoff and much of the financial community, prove that many of our most respected businesspeople have acted irresponsibly. These scandals and the coinciding economic turmoil demonstrate that we cannot afford to place our resources—and our children's futures—in the hands of unregulated mercenaries. The undermining of organizations and laws that once protected the public interest has been disastrous; some of the most obvious and onerous examples, discussed previously in this book, include:

- The deregulation of the energy, transportation, communications, banking, finance, and insurance sectors

- The abandonment of caps on usurious interest rates

- The acceptance of false accounting standards that exclude externalities

- The creation of international agreements, such as NAFTA, CAFTA, and other "free market" zones around the globe that have promoted licenses to plunder

- The imposition of Structural Adjustment Programs (SAPs) on other nations and the resulting privatization of their resources

These illustrate that, in Shuar terms, we have killed mating birds and continued to utilize trails that are annihilating ecosystems.

Fortunately, the calamitous consequences are forcing us to finally understand our folly. Even some of the most conservative economists now conclude that deregulation and the other strategies that gave businesses unprecedented freedoms are major factors contributing to the worst recession since the 1930s and that rules governing corporations serve an essential function. Rather than inhibiting economic expansion, such a body of regulations establishes parameters for long-term growth.

We have seen that executives are human and capable of succumbing to the temptation of abusing their powers. On the other hand, history demonstrates that when rules mandate serving the common good, corporations and their bosses do exactly that.

Perhaps no public figure was more aware of this than Teddy Roosevelt. He assumed the presidency in 1901, after a financial collapse that was caused by corporate abuses, mass mergers, and the robber barons who had sought and won deregulation. He dissolved monopolistic corporations and pushed through laws that regulated the railroads and other industries.

Roosevelt had little tolerance for business and government leaders who were not committed to the common good. In a Labor Day speech delivered in 1903, he said:

> The death-knell of the republic had rung as soon as the active power became lodged in the hands of those who sought, not to do justice to all citizens, rich and poor alike, but to stand for one special class and for its interests as opposed to the interests of others.[1]

He recognized the dangers of unregulated businesses and of executives who were driven solely by a desire to increase their power and profits. Roosevelt's Pulitzer Prize–winning biographer, Edmund Morris, speculated about actions Roosevelt might take if he occupied the White House today:

> [H]e would want to do something about Microsoft, since he had been passionate about monopoly from the moment he entered politics. Although no single trust a hundred years ago approached the monolithic immensity of Mr. Gates' empire, the Northern Securities merger of 1901 created the greatest transport combine in the world, controlling commerce from Chicago to China.
>
> T.R. busted it. In doing so he burnished himself with instant glory as the champion of American individual enterprise against corporate "malefactors of great wealth."[2]

Roosevelt understood, however, that clamping down on greedy business operators was only the first step. The process of regulation had to go beyond that. In addition to the triage necessary to cure the nation's economic ills, he believed that government had a responsibility to protect future generations. He called for a national health plan and advocated a strategy to ensure that citizens would forever be the beneficiaries of the country's natural resources. In a move the Shuar would undoubtedly applaud, he created the Bureau of Forestry and signed into existence five new national parks, eighteen national monuments, and millions of acres of national forest.[3]

We know now what Roosevelt knew then, that recovery from severe economic turmoil requires long-term innovation. The solutions must include responses that endure for decades to come.

Reinstating the types of regulations that for more than half a century protected us from another 1929 Crash is essential. Yet it is not sufficient. The world has changed radically since the time of the Great Depression. Global populations have more than tripled; the depletion of resources has increased at accelerating rates, as has pollution, toxicity, and species' extinctions. Ships' crews discover huge garbage dumps in the middle of the oceans. Astronauts confront it in outer space. Every living system is in decline, and every one of them is declining at ever-increasing speeds. Today we are awash in a sea of problems so severe that they have pushed us to the brink of disaster.

Although we need the modern equivalent of the Glass-Steagall Act, the Bank Holding Company Act, and so many of the others that were dropped after 1980, we must not stop there. This nation deserves a whole new set of rules and regulations that ensure a sustainable, just, and peaceful world for my grandson and all his brothers and sisters everywhere. It deserves an accounting system that internalizes the externalities and in doing so, ensures that the most socially and environmentally responsible businesses enjoy a competitive edge over others—instead of vice versa.

The cancer that lurks beneath this economic crisis will not be cured by merely addressing the problems of the banking, insurance, and auto industries. Like a patient after his cancerous lung has been removed who must quit smoking if he wants a healthy life, our long-term health depends on addressing the underlying causes. The goal of maximizing profits regardless of environmental and social costs must become a relic of history.

Barack Obama's election as president signaled that a majority of voters rejected the principles that had determined U.S. policy for more than a third of a century. His calls for a "Credit Cardholders' Bill of Rights" that imposes tighter regulation on the credit card industry, along with tougher rules on auto emissions and mileage, and a new regulatory commission to oversee financial products and services including banks, mortgage providers, and mutual funds—all of these measures indicate an important philosophical shift.

The danger is that we will become so wrapped up in debates over these and other issues that focus on the current economic crises that we will forget to address the systemic problems. There is the very real possibility that partisan politics and special interests will distract us from enacting the types of laws that would rid us once and for all of the mutant virus and offer instead a healthy form of capitalism.

We must not let that happen. We cannot afford to be lulled into complacency. Or allow indicators of "good news" like temporary increases in the stock market, lower oil prices, and payoffs of loans by bailed-out banks to soothe us into believing that things have returned to "normal." It is essential to keep in mind that "normal" led us into this disaster, and it will quickly propel us into a much worse one, despite the possibility of short-term recoveries, unless we change the parameters. The old "normal" where 5 percent of the globe's people consume 25 percent of its resources and half the population verges on starvation must be rejected. A true replacement is called for. Our planet shouts at us to take bold steps. Let us, the voters, the consumers, the ones whose children will have to live with the policies implemented right now, insist that our leaders show the courage to truly lead.

Most of us consider the legislation of rules and regulations to be the job of our elected officials. While technically this is true, those officials look to us to guide their decisions. As consumers, it is our job to let the corporations know that we want better controls. As voters, it is our responsibility to demand legislation that protects us and our progeny from the types of abuses that are causing so much suffering around the planet today.

We have the power to make it happen. The only requirement: that we focus on our individual passions and talents.

CHAPTER 24

Honoring Your Passion

If there had been more space in the Politico.com [web page], I would have told the story that Hillary Clinton told me when I met with her in the White House: When FDR met with labor leaders in 1934, after four hours of meeting, he said the following—"You've convinced me that you are right. Now, go out there and FORCE ME TO DO IT." What he meant, Hillary explained to me, was that the pressures on a president to stay with the status quo and the forces of the economic and political elites of the country are enormous, so that even when a president wishes to move in a different direction, he needs to be able to point to forces from the progressive world that are equally vociferous and pushing him in the direction he wished to go.

—*Source:* "A Note from Rabbi Michael Lerner" entitled "Obama's Nonideological Pragmatism Will Backfire,"[1] discussing an article he published on www.Politico.com on May 20, 2009.[2]

A theme repeated throughout this book is that we the people must make it happen. We have to look to ourselves to create a sustainable, just, and peaceful planet. The point Hillary Clinton made to Rabbi

Lerner is exactly that. We cannot sit back and expect President Obama, or anyone else, to rescue us. Our political leaders count on us to demand that they do the right thing.

Abraham Lincoln eloquently admonished us to make sure that "government of the people, by the people, for the people, shall not perish from the earth" in his Gettysburg Address. Such a government requires active participation from its citizens. Or it will perish.

What is true for politicians is also true for business leaders. They may try to influence our shopping habits through various promotional methods, but in the end we make the decisions. The success or failure of their businesses depends on us. FDR's advice to the unions about how they should push—help—him applies to us and corporate executives as well. We need to hear their plea: "FORCE ME TO DO IT."

An essential ingredient in all of this is passion. In order for those labor leaders to get through to FDR, they had to be moved by passion. Lincoln recognized that he had to fire the nation's passions. His famous address ended in an emotional call for impassioned action:

> It is rather for us to be here dedicated to the great task remaining before us—that from these honored dead we take increased devotion to that cause for which they gave the last full measure of devotion—that we here highly resolve that these dead shall not have died in vain—that this nation, under God, shall have a new birth of freedom.

Passion has made the difference throughout history. It won the American Revolution. Carried the day at Normandy. Spurred the civil rights movement. *Passion* by definition is "an intense or overpowering emotion such as love, joy, hatred, or anger" (*Encarta World*

English Dictionary). The important point for each of us as individuals is to recognize our passions—whether we consider them "positive" such as love and joy or "negative" like hatred and anger—and then to direct the energy they generate in ways that effect the results we desire. Case in point:

Rainforest Action Network (RAN) has convinced some of the world's most powerful companies—including Bank of America, Boise Cascade, Citigroup, Chase, Home Depot, Kinko's, and Staples—to change their policies toward cutting trees. A few years back RAN went up against the Mitsubishi corporate family, at the time considered one of the world's most destructive loggers of tropical forests. In a bitter campaign, a Mitsubishi executive faced off against RAN's founder Randy Hayes.

Ultimately, RAN emerged victorious. Mitsubishi companies signed an agreement that committed them to "ecological sustainability and social responsibility," and they pledged to implement fourteen specific steps for fulfilling their commitment.

Several months later, I attended a weekend conference in California, along with both the Mitsubishi executive and Randy. Following an initial, rather stiff greeting, they studiously avoided each other. Late Saturday afternoon Randy and I decided to head up to a hot tub at the top of a cliff overlooking the Pacific, share a few beers, and exchange stories about our adventures in the Amazon. We were shocked to find someone else already there.

The Mitsubishi executive grinned awkwardly up from the bubbles, raised his own beer, and invited us to join him.

I have to admit that I felt very nervous. Here I was, perched high above the Pacific, alone except for two other men who had been archenemies, naked, in a hot tub, drinking beer. I wondered what would happen next.

After some small talk about the conference, the Mitsubishi executive raised his can and said to Randy, "I need to thank you."

He went on to explain that he and other people at Mitsubishi had wanted to change company policies toward forests, but they had not dared to, for fear of losing their jobs. "Your protesters and ads forced the issue," he continued. "Someone pointed out that our responsibilities shouldn't stop with today's stockholders; they should include the stockholders' kids, our kids. RAN gave us an opportunity. We convinced ourselves, our company, to do the right thing."

As the three of us continued talking, the executive kept referring to the passion of the RAN people. "That's what impressed me most," he said. "The zeal, the fervor of those individuals—young and old! We all felt it. It was contagious."

Many of those volunteers were extremely angry at Mitsubishi for cutting forests. However, rather than directing this "negative" energy at something destructive (for example, hurling Molotov cocktails at corporate headquarters) or self-destructive (such as anesthetizing themselves with drugs or alcohol), they channeled their collective emotions into activities that achieved their desired results. Their enthusiasm persuaded one of the world's most powerful conglomerates to change its policies.

Since then I have heard many similar stories. One person's passion can move other people to transform themselves—or, in the case of executives, their corporations. This is especially true when the other people, or executives, know deep in their hearts that they want change. And today, we all understand that we desire something vastly different from this world of predatory capitalism. Whether in the Oval Office or a corporate boardroom, men and women in decision-making positions do not want climate change to sink Florida beneath the ocean; nor do they want any of the other ill effects caused by pollution, the wanton depletion of resources, and abusive labor practices. However, until they are pushed, they feel powerless. The heartfelt commitment of consumers and activists is their tipping point.

"Passion has changed my life," Lynne Twist told a group of us. The founder of the Soul of Money Institute—whose mission is to empower people to realign the acquisition and allocation of financial resources with their most passionately held values—and author of the bestselling book *The Soul of Money*, Lynne followed her passions and moved to Ecuador in early 2008 with her husband Bill. I had taken the two of them to that country in the early 1990s, and as a result they founded The Pachamama Alliance (TPA), a nonprofit organization that works closely with indigenous people and is dedicated to preserving the earth's rain forests and to creating a new global vision of equity and sustainability for people everywhere. She, Bill, and TPA's staff in Ecuador coordinated a successful campaign with the Ecuadorian government and other NGOs to include in Ecuador's new constitution a groundbreaking legal concept that grants fundamental rights to nature and the natural environment.

Now, four months later, Lynne had led a group of TPA supporters deep into the Amazon to celebrate the new year with the Achuar tribe; we were floating casually down a river, watching a pod of pink dolphins that was swimming nearby and had apparently assembled to watch us.

"The passions of so many Ecuadorians is what made this amazing constitution possible," Lynne continued. "The enthusiasm, drive, and talents of President Rafael Correa, combined with those of indigenous leaders, created a true miracle—one that will serve as a model for other countries and future generations for years to come."

It is fair to say that passion is behind every major event. It has been the driving force of history. However, for it to be truly effective, passion requires something else that Lynne alluded to: talent. And just as each of us has passion, we also have special talents: personality traits, skills, and other abilities developed over the years. The real secret to changing the world—or, for that matter, being successful at anything—is to apply our talents in ways that satisfy our passions.

To cite a personal example: My passion for writing started when I was an only child growing up in rural New Hampshire, as a means of dealing with loneliness. I had a deep admiration for authors who took a stand, like Paine, Jefferson, Thoreau, and many of the columnists I read in newspapers. I became editor in chief of my prep school paper, and I fought for changes in the school's draconian disciplinary policies. Writing offered a way to redirect the anger I felt over injustices committed in South Africa, Selma, Alabama, and on Indian reservations, as well as at my school. It moved me away from self-destructive actions into activities that could generate change. Today, I am most happy when I write to promote worthy causes.

Passion is powerful. It is infectious. It drives the world. One person's passion quickly spreads. Name people who have influenced you—in literature, music, painting, theater, sports, or politics—and you will find they have applied their talents in ways that promoted their passions.

Ordinary people filled with passion accomplish extraordinary tasks. Growing up in New Hampshire, I had no idea that African Americans had to ride in the back of the bus in some parts of my country, until Rosa Parks showed me—and mobilized a civil rights movement that became global. I had no idea that the DDT we sprayed on the marsh behind our house to control mosquitoes also killed fish, birds, and squirrels until Rachel Carson wrote *Silent Spring*. I was pushed around by a bully, until my third grade teacher, Mrs. Schnare, convinced me to stand up to him, which taught me about courage and the importance of not allowing others to get away with abusive behavior. I did not appreciate the powerful impact Tom Paine's *Common Sense* had on American colonists until I studied with a high school English teacher named Richard

Davis. Or that George Washington and John Hancock, two of the wealthiest men in the colonies, would have been hanged as traitors if we had lost the Revolution, until I listened to a history teacher named Jack Woodbury.

All these people followed their own paths. Their only shared traits were that they all had passion and they all were talented teachers in one way or another; they impacted people. Some made the history books. Of those who did not—Schnare, Davis, and Woodbury—I personally can say that, without them, I would not have written these pages.

We can be grateful that Paine did not try to lead armies and Washington did not write pamphlets. The former had a passion and talent for pamphlet writing, the latter for leading men. Ardent women, like Martha Washington, organized themselves into groups to make clothes for soldiers on the front lines. Hunters became sharpshooters. Fishermen joined the fledgling navy. Along the way, their example motivated others. They were all teachers. Inspirations to future generations.

You too have passion. And talents. You are a teacher. You can inspire. The opportunity is there every time you speak to anyone, purchase something (or choose not to), or send an e-mail. You teach through words and actions.

The questions for you are these: What are your passions? Talents? What will bring you the greatest sense of accomplishment? Satisfaction and joy?

Whether you are a student, dentist, plumber, housewife, or something else, you can talk to your friends, family, and clients about the issues, join organizations that represent your passions, send e-mails, use materials that are environmentally and socially responsible, support politicians who take actions oriented to benefit future generations, vote in the marketplace for companies committed to doing the right thing, and accomplish objectives you have dared only to dream about until now.

It all starts with recognizing your power. You initiate it by knowing that you have the ability to sit at the front of a bus, inspire a young person to stand up to a bully, and talk about the courage of our Founding Fathers and Mothers. Like every one of your personal heroes, you sometimes hesitate, falter, make mistakes, and learn from your errors. You too can change the world. Commit to honoring your passion and acknowledging your power. When you combine yours with the passions and talents of everyone else who reads this page, miracles will happen.

Together we can create a world that is free of the mutant virus. Like Parks, Carson, Paine, the Washingtons, Schnare, Davis, Woodbury, the hunters, and the fishermen, we can each walk a separate path. The important thing is that we all head toward the same destination—a sustainable, just, and peaceful world.

Conclusion

"You've played around in the Amazon," Omar Torrijos chided me late one afternoon in 1978 as we strolled outside Panama's Presidential Palace, along an ancient wall built to defend the city against pirates; "but you haven't experienced real jungle until you've tried to hack your way through . . ." he pointed across the bay, "the Darién Gap."

I could see nothing but water and a low, misty coastline, but I knew it was there, off in the distance, beyond my vision—a vast green jumble of vegetation. In those days, the Darién stretched over the mountains and swamps that separate Colombia from Panama, South America from Central America. All my life I had heard it described in ominous terms, a dense rain forest of nightmarish perils, a mysterious no-man's land crawling with deadly bushmaster pit vipers, jaguars, crocodiles, and hostile natives—the only spot between northern Alaska and the southern tip of Argentina the Pan-American Highway had not penetrated.

"Even Noriega," Torrijos continued, referring to his chief of military intelligence, "isn't crazy enough to go in on foot. He hunts wild boars in the Darién—from a helicopter!"

Now, more than three decades after that conversation with Omar, I was driving through the "impenetrable" Darién, totally shocked by the devastation surrounding me. It was July 2009, and the luxuriant rain forest that previously covered tens of thousands of square miles had disappeared. In its place were scattered pastures populated by scrawny herds of cattle. The once-pristine rivers reeked of cow manure. The eroded hillsides oozed mud. I had been told that all that remained of contiguous jungle was a mere twelve miles at the point where the Pan-American Highway will likely soon connect Panama and Colombia. The rest had been ravaged by cattle ranchers and lumber companies, the wild animals butchered by poachers. Torrijos had been assassinated, and Noriega was rotting in a U.S. prison.

"Until now, what has saved that last patch," Nathan Gray, my driver and host, advised me, "is that the United Nations claims it's the only barrier preventing hoof-and-mouth disease from spreading out of South America to the north."

I peered through the windshield in the direction of that remaining remnant, a mirage that faded into the horizon. "A microcosm for a world created by predatory capitalists," I murmured.

Nathan shot me a look but said nothing as he maneuvered his four-wheel drive pickup truck along the muddy dirt road. It struck me that this man beside me was the opposite of those predatory capitalists; Nathan Gray represented the new type of capitalists who collectively are leading us away from the mutant virus that has brought us to the precipice of economic collapse. He and the others bear the torches that illuminate a path toward a healthier form of capitalism based on creating an ecologically sustainable planet.

I recalled another day with Omar Torrijos. We were standing at the rail of a yacht docked at Contadora Island when he introduced me to the two words that had come to represent the people who have driven our economy to ruins. He warned that unless we stopped the *predatory capitalists*, global markets would go into shock, and he added, "Don't allow yourself to be hoodwinked."

I had fallen into the trap. Most of us had. It appeared that Nathan Gray was one of the few who had never been hoodwinked.

He was a founder in 1973 of Oxfam America, a highly acclaimed international assistance organization based in Boston. He started the nonprofit Earth Train in 1990 as an international youth leadership training organization that promotes community development in Third World countries and that also pioneered partnerships between nonprofits and for-profits as a way to raise money from socially conscious investors. In 2001, along with Rainforest Capital, LLC (a socially conscious investment company), the Kuna General Congress (representing the indigenous culture), the Fundación Danilo Perez (founded by the Grammy-winning Panamanian jazz musician), the BioMuseo of Panama, and a number of individual Panamanians, Nathan established the Mamoní Valley Preserve in what had once been rain forest on the edge of the Darién Province.

Emilio Mariscal tapped my shoulder. Sitting behind Nathan in the pickup truck's two-seater cabin, he was the preserve's director of agroforestry. "Over there," he said, "is one of my teams of planters." He pointed at a half dozen men off in the distance, bent over, tenderly placing saplings into the earth. Emilio is a highly regarded forestry and sustainable agriculture expert who served from 2002 to 2007 as a lead field coordinator for the Native Species Reforestation Project in Panama, a program of Harvard University's Center for Tropical Forest Science, the Smithsonian Tropical Research Institute, and the Yale School of Forestry.

"How many planters do you have?" asked Llyn Roberts, who was sitting beside Emilio. She is the director of Dream Change, a nonprofit I founded back in the early 1990s that is dedicated to preserving indigenous wisdom and shifting global consciousness. Llyn has lived and worked with indigenous people in Asia and in Central and South America, teaches workshops on transformation, and is the author of several books, including *The Good Remembering* and *Shamaic Reiki*. Nathan had asked her and Dream Change to spearhead the spiritual branch of Earth Train and to facilitate the inclusion of local indigenous cultures—the Embera and Kuna—into its Panamanian programs.

"Twelve right now," Emilio answered. "We'll plant 30,000 trees this year—all native species that will bring this place back in a decade or so."

"That hollow," Nathan interjected, pointing at an indentation in the scrubby pasture off to our left, "used to be a wetland swarming with migratory birds. Once the trees reestablish themselves, the wetlands will regenerate, and the birds'll return. Today, this preserve encompasses 10,000 acres, but it is positioned to protect over 150,000 acres of biologically diverse lands in Kuna territory." He had explained to me during previous telephone conversations that the land purchases were capitalized through private investments. The business model for this preserve is a creative combination of international private-sector financing, community development, environmental research, and grassroots organization.

"We're not trying to drive local people off the land," Nathan continued, as we bounced through the potholes. "Without preaching, we're quietly demonstrating to these cattle ranchers that they'll be far better off allowing this land to go back to rain forest and selling its natural products sustainably: hardwoods, fruits, vegetables, orchids, ornamentals, groundcovers, and ecohospitality. We set an example through our research and teaching facility, Centro Madroño, and we even provide the ranchers with financing to convert if they need it. We buy land, although mostly from absentee ranchers and only when it is the sole option for getting cows off it. Our goal is to help everyone create a new forest- and watershed-based economy."

Nathan parked the truck at the top of a hill and pointed down into a beautiful valley formed by the Mamoní River. "That's where we're going to build Junglewood, a performing and visual arts center." A joint venture between Earth Train and Fundación Danilo Perez in cooperation with Boston's Berklee College of Music, Junglewood is loosely modeled after Tanglewood, the summer home of the Boston Symphony Orchestra in the Berkshire mountains of western Massachusetts. "Danilo's friends Wayne Shorter and Herbie Hancock are among several popular musicians who are committed to helping him realize his dream of turning this place into Mother Nature's ultimate tropical rehearsal space and a music camp for kids."

He shifted into four-wheel drive and headed along the ridge. "We're engaging top architects and artisans to create a place where accomplished artists and talented kids can reconnect with nature. Here's where they'll come to work on new compositions and use their music to inspire and teach folks from all over and form bridges with indigenous and local people. Jane Goodall will arrive for a visit later this year. She's considering setting up a center in Panama to teach teachers. This evening you'll meet Dr. Catherine Lindell, a Michigan State professor who is using this place as a living laboratory to study the effects of land-cover restoration on the behavior of birds." He grinned. "Aren't you glad I persuaded you to come?"

It was a reference to my attempts to resist him. When he first called me, I had been facing an August deadline for completing this book, and I did not see how I could fit a trip to Panama's jungles into my schedule. Nathan had assured me that I would understand once I got there.

The night before, at an event right after my arrival in this country where I had once spent so much time as an EHM, Nathan had been proven right. Earth Train hosted a reception for Llyn and me. It was held on the rooftop garden of their offices in the colonial section of Panama City—just a couple of blocks from the Presidential Palace and the old wall where Omar Torrijos and I had strolled that day all those many years ago. We were joined by Kuna chiefs and NGO leaders, as well as Danilo Perez and many other dignitaries, and we were treated to a slide show presentation for the new "Bridge of Life" BioMuseo that will be housed in a building designed by world-renowned architect Frank O. Gehry and constructed on a promontory of land that used to be part of the U.S.-occupied Canal Zone.

Behind us were the lights of ships anchored in the bay, waiting to sail from the Pacific, through the canal, into the Atlantic; and in front of us were slides flashing on a screen while we were told by the museum executive director, Lider Sucre, that Panama had been formed as a bridge of life between North and South America around 3 million years ago. Before that time, the two oceans had been joined. Panama's creation had changed everything. The land masses were united and the oceans divided. The flora, fauna, and environments of both land and water were forever altered. The entire planet was impacted by the changes in global ocean currents and climate.

Later that night, as I walked back to the apartment where I was staying, through the ancient winding streets, an observation by one of the Kuna elders kept running through my mind. "Here in Panama," he said, "the Great Creator made a bridge across the oceans. Then the Yankees came and tore a hole in that bridge with a canal. Since then we have all been divided—people from nature, people from each other, North from South, East from West. Everything went crazy. It is up to us to build a new type of bridge."

Nathan drove the pickup through a small gate and into the Centro Madroño, a cluster of small open-air cottages and a couple of large meeting lodges scattered amidst one of the preserved sections of luxuriant rain forest. After showers and a brief rest, Llyn, Emilio, Nathan, and I made our way to dinner. A group had assembled in the dining hall. The diversity of the people was representative of the organization. There was a young leader of the Emberá, Raul Mezua, and one from the Kuna, Toniel Edman; their two tribes are traditional enemies that have now united to try to save their threatened lands and cultures, and they had become comrades in this crusade to reverse the destruction of the Darién ecoregion. Also present were a former local cattle rancher turned environmentalist, Rolando Toribio; a young lawyer, Carlos Andres, who had decided to forgo the big bucks in favor of doing something that "makes my heart sing"; and a representative from Global Brigades, the world's largest student-led health and sustainable development organization, Allen Gula.

During the ensuing conversations, Llyn referred to the Kuna elder's observation at the reception on the roof overlooking the bay the evening before. "This concept of building a new bridge," she told the group, "is part of the Prophecy of the Eagle and Condor."

"Please," Nathan coaxed, "recite it."

"As far as we can tell," she replied, "this prophecy originated in the Amazon over 2,000 years ago. It traveled up into the Andes, then across this isthmus, influencing the legends of the Maya, Aztecs, Hopi, and many North American tribes. In summary, it says that during ancient times human societies divided into two groups. The Condor People represented 'the path of the heart,' adhering to the ideals of the deep feminine, opting for lifestyles that create peaceful, sustainable environments favorable for giving birth, raising families, and passing knowledge about the natural world to their children. The Eagle People followed 'the path of the mind,' advocating values we associate with masculine traits, creating societies that develop technologies for conquering other tribes and dominating nature. According to this prophecy, the two paths would converge during the Fourth Pachacuti—'Pachacuti' is a Quechua/Incan word designating a 500-year period—beginning in the 1490s. There would be wars, terrible violence, and the Eagle would drive the Condor to the verge of extinction."

Llyn glanced around the table. "Of course, we know that is exactly what happened after Columbus's voyage. The prophecy was realized; the industrial cultures of the world practically destroyed the indigenous ones. Then, according to the prophecy, 500 years later, starting in the 1990s, a new Pachacuti would begin, the fifth. It is said to be a time when the Condor and Eagle have the opportunity to reunite. This is not a given, as we must make it happen, but the opportunity exists for the Eagle and Condor—mind and heart—to soar together in the same sky, dancing, mating, and restoring balance." She glanced at Toniel and Raul and then, spreading her arms, embraced everyone at the table. "It is happening. We're seeing it in so many parts of the world: the Condor people sharing their wisdom and the Eagle people trying to repair the damage we have wrought. Look at what's going on right here."

"We are that bridge we heard about during the slide show last night," Christine Del Vecchio, an Earth Train organizer, added. "We in Panama are dancing the Eagle-Condor dance."

"The Mamoní Valley Preserve" I said, "is a place to incubate dreams. The old dream was based on exploiting—conquering—nature and people. The new one is about living in harmony." I went on to tell them that I had always thought the prophecy is about a sort of evolution, elevating human cultures to a new level of consciousness where heart and mind are truly integrated. "This current economic crisis," I said, "is no fluke. It had to happen to shake us awake."

The incredible vision that is materializing in the Mamoní Valley Preserve was juxtaposed by the political turmoil sweeping another Central American country in July 2009. Everyone I talked with in Panama was convinced that the military coup that had overthrown the democratically elected president of Honduras, Manuel Zelaya, had been engineered by two U.S. companies, with CIA support. Earlier in the year Chiquita Brands International, Inc. (formerly United Fruit), and Dole Food Company, Inc., had severely criticized President Zelaya for advocating an increase of 60 percent in Honduras's minimum wage, claiming that the policy would cut into corporate profits.

Memories are short in the United States but not in places like Panama. Whether I chatted with men planting trees in the Darién ecoregion, taxi drivers, waiters and shopkeepers in Panama City, or the movers and shakers I met at the rooftop reception, I kept hearing people who claimed that it was a matter of record that Chiquita (United Fruit) and the CIA had toppled Guatemala's democratically elected president Jacobo Arbenz in 1954 and that International Telephone & Telegraph (ITT), Henry Kissinger, and the CIA had brought down Chile's Salvador Allende in 1973. These people were certain that Haiti's president Jean-Bertrand Aristide had been ousted by the CIA in 2004 because he proposed a minimum wage increase, like President Zelaya's.

I was told by a Panamanian bank vice president who wanted to remain anonymous, "Every multinational knows that if Honduras raises its hourly rate, the rest of Latin America and the Caribbean will have to follow. Haiti and Honduras have always set the bottom line for minimum wages. The big companies are determined to stop what they call a 'leftist revolt' in this hemisphere. In throwing out Zelaya, they are sending frightening messages to all the other presidents who are trying to raise the living standards of their people."

It did not take much imagination to envision the turmoil sweeping through every Latin American capital. There had been a collective sigh of relief at Barack Obama's election in the United States, a sense of hope that the empire in the North would finally exhibit compassion toward its southern neighbors, that the unfair trade agreements, privatizations, draconian IMF Structural Adjustment Programs, and threats of military intervention would slow down and perhaps even fade away. Now, that optimism was turning sour.

The cozy relationship between Honduras's military coup leaders and the corporatocracy was confirmed a couple of days after my arrival in Panama. England's *Guardian* ran an article announcing that "two of the Honduran coup government's top advisers have close ties to the U.S. secretary of state. One is Lanny Davis, an influential lobbyist who was a personal lawyer for President Bill Clinton and also campaigned for Hillary. . . . The other hired gun for the coup government that has deep Clinton ties is [lobbyist] Bennett Ratcliff."[1]

Democracy Now! broke the news that Chiquita was represented by a powerful Washington law firm, Covington & Burling LLP, and its consultant, McLarty Associates.[2] President Obama's attorney general, Eric Holder, had been a Covington partner and a defender of Chiquita when the company was accused of hiring "assassination squads" in Colombia (Chiquita was found guilty, admitting that it had paid organizations listed by the U.S. government as terrorist groups "for protection" and agreeing in 2004 to a $25 million fine).[3]

George W. Bush's U.N. ambassador, John Bolton, a former Covington lawyer, had fiercely opposed Latin American leaders who fought for their peoples' rights to larger shares of the profits derived from their resources. After leaving the government in 2006, Bolton became involved with the Project for the New American Century, the Council for National Policy, and a number of other programs that promote corporate hegemony in Honduras and elsewhere. McLarty Vice Chairman John Negroponte was the U.S. ambassador to Honduras from 1981 to 1985, a former deputy secretary of state, director of national intelligence, and U.S. representative to the United Nations. He played a major role in the U.S.-backed Contras' secret war against Nicaragua's Sandinista government, and he has consistently opposed the policies of the democratically elected pro-reform Latin American presidents.[4] These men symbolize the insidious power of the corporatocracy, its bipartisan composition, and the fact that the Obama administration has been sucked in.

Holder, Bolton, and Negroponte are among the more visible

representatives of a cadre of influential men and women who are determined to maintain a status quo that has brought us to the perilous edge of global collapse. They and the many others who serve them trace their heritage back to the beginnings of EHM and jackal operations in Iran and Indonesia. They prefer to implement their policies quietly, behind closed doors, but they do not hesitate to draw on the military when all else fails—or when they feel that there simply is not enough time for the more subtle approaches. The *Los Angeles Times* went to the heart of this matter when, on July 23, 2009, it concluded the following:

> What happened in Honduras is a classic Latin American coup in another sense: Gen. Romeo Vasquez, who led it, is an alumnus of the United States' School of the Americas (renamed the Western Hemisphere Institute for Security Cooperation). The school is best known for producing Latin American officers who have committed major human rights abuses, including military coups.[5]

As I sat in my little open-air cottage in the Darién ecoregion in July 2009 reading the articles about Honduras, I kept recalling how vehemently Omar Torrijos had opposed this type of clandestine empire building. "It degrades the United States," he said. "It makes a mockery of democracy." He himself had attended the School of the Americas (located in the U.S.-occupied Panama Canal Zone in those days), and he understood its sinister implications. He referred to it as the "School of the Assassins." Once he became Panama's head of government, he demanded that the United States remove the school from his country; as part of the Canal Treaty, the Pentagon transferred it to Fort Benning, Georgia.

Late one afternoon, I wandered along a jungle trail and into a clearing at the top of a hill. The Mamoní River snaked through the valley below. I sat down on a log and thought about the classic war that had pitted supporters of John Maynard Keynes against those of Milton Friedman. The latter's victory had changed the world—and brought on the crisis we now face. It seemed that today, here, on this relatively small stretch of land between North and South America, a new war was raging.

One battle, in Honduras, was making headlines. It was being waged with the traditional corporatocracy weapons: a military coup to replace a legitimately elected president who refused to succumb to EHM bribes and threats, a U.S. public relations blitz similar to ones previously employed to justify imperialism in the name of democracy in so many countries, and a battery of extremely influential lawyers and lobbyists whose cannons were aimed at the courts, Congress, and the United Nations to defend Chiquita, Dole, and their allies. The word had been broadcast across network television and the mainstream newspapers in the United States that President Zelaya had tried to usurp the electoral process by announcing that his government would conduct a poll to determine popular sentiments regarding the extension of presidential term limits. Hundreds of millions of dollars had poured into the media and the halls of Washington to keep the public ignorant about the real reason behind the military takeover: President Zelaya had the audacity to expose the terrible working conditions on the agribusiness plantations, the suffering and diseases, the low wages and malnutrition among those who raise the bananas and pineapples that grace our breakfast tables, and that he had the integrity not to bend to corruption but instead to demand something better for his people. Honduras was a battle fought to defend the mutant virus form of capitalism.

Another battle, the one in Panama, was quietly being waged with a new array of weapons: seeds, hoes, and sustainable agricultural techniques, socially conscious capital, music, a melding of indigenous wisdom with scientific research, and a squadron of former cattle ranchers, community organizers, ecologists, artists, writers, NGOs, web designers, a new wave of lawyers, and people, young and old, from many other walks of life who were coming together to take their place in forging an innovative, healthy form of capitalism.

The old war between Keynes and Friedman might seem a relic of the past, the recession its tombstone; however, the corporatocracy was not standing quietly beside the grave. Their candidate had not won the U.S. presidential race, but their people had quickly infiltrated some of the most influential offices in the White House, Federal Reserve, Pentagon, and State Department. Their bankers had marched back to Wall Street and were once again paying themselves unearned bonuses. Although the IMF had fallen into disrepute in the early and mid-2000s, the G-20 countries had infused it with more than triple its previous capital and awarded it new mandates for power in 2008 and 2009.

And, as if to let the world know that the recession, the tombstone, was merely a warning and not symbolic of a real death, the EHMs and jackals had drawn a line in the sands of Honduras.

We are all arrayed along that line. It is up to each of us to decide. Do we want a world ruled by a few billionaires, intent on controlling the planet's resources with the goal of serving their increasingly voracious appetites? Do we want more debt, privatization, and markets where robber barons elevate themselves above the rules and regulations that apply to the rest of us? Accounting systems that fail to record the most egregious costs? Magazine cover "heroes" who exploit their workers, pay fortunes to lawyers and lobbyists to defend the status quo, and ship their money to overseas tax havens? Do we want to buy from corporations that finance the overthrow of democratically elected governments? Undermine our own presidents and elected officials? Do we want to raise our children on a planet where less than 5 percent of the population consumes more than 25 percent of the resources, less than 10 percent of that 5 percent control the assets, and roughly half the world lives in poverty? Where violence continues to rise, and our militaristic tactics against "terrorism" force us into a constant state of siege?

Or do we want something else? Do we want a world envisioned by the organizations that are striving to create a socially and environmentally responsible economy—the type of organizations we find at Green Festivals, local markets, in stores and on websites that are committed to the triple bottom line? Do we want a world where the models for our children are the founders and managers of institutions that restore rain forests and polluted lakes, promote sustainable energy, and help starving people feed themselves? Where no one is denied medical care and the right to live out the last days of his or her life in dignity? In short, do we want to break the old pattern, rid ourselves of the viral form of predatory capitalism that is failing us so badly, and bequeath a world to future generations that reflects the ideals of true democracy, a world headed toward sustainable, just, and peaceful societies for us all?

This choice does not lie with Barack Obama. Or John McCain. Or any other politician.

The choice is ours.

Acknowledgments

My deepest thanks to:

My literary agent, Paul Fedorko, for presenting the idea for this book to me and helping shape it—as well as for all his hard work, enduring friendship, and the sage advice he has given me over all these years.

My editor at Random House/Broadway Books, Roger Scholl, for untangling the Gordian knots in the original manuscript, his brilliant wordsmithing, and his willingness to sacrifice precious vacation hours to the tedious job of editing and reediting so that we could release this book on a timely basis.

My publicist, Peg Booth, for all her support during these many years, including scheduling interviews and events in ways that allowed me to meet this book's tight schedule.

My wife, Winifred, for reading large sections of the manuscript, for offering invaluable advice on how to improve them, and for being such a wonderful partner, mother of Jessica, and grandmother of Grant.

My son-in-law Daniel Miller for developing my website, guiding me through the pathways of the Internet labyrinth, and impressing upon me the importance of social networking as the modern equivalent of the Gutenberg press.

Kathleen McMullen Coady for helping me understand the power of that word first expressed to me by Omar Torrijos and suggesting it as the title: "Hoodwinked."

And all the people and organizations mentioned in these pages who facilitated my recent trips to China, Ecuador, Iceland, Nicaragua, Panama, Tibet, the colleges, universities, conferences, and seminars, and whose ideas have played such an essential role in helping me understand the insidious nature of the problem we now face and formulate the solutions presented herein.

Notes

INTRODUCTION

1. For additional information and statistics, see Michael Lewis, "Wall Street on the Tundra," *Vanity Fair*, April 2009, pp. 142–147; 173–177; and Ian Parker, Letter from Reykjavik, "Lost: After Financial Disaster, Icelanders Reassess Their Identity," *New Yorker*, March 9, 2009, pp. 39–47.

2. Ibid.

CHAPTER 1

1. Rodrigue Tremblay, "The Dance of the Trillions to Shore up Banks, Bankers, and Gamblers," *Global Research*, Centre for Research on Globalization, March 26, 2009, http://www.globalresearch.ca/index.php?context=va&aid=12918.

2. "The Crisis and How to Deal with It," *New York Review of Books*, June 11, 2009, pp. 73–76.

3. U.S. Bureau of Labor Statistics, Economic News Release: "Employment Situation Summary," May 28, 2009, http://www.bls.gov; Lucia Mutikani, "U.S. Economy Tumbles Steeply in First Quarter," Reuters, April 29, 2009 (accessed May 27, 2009), http://www.reuters.com/article/newsOne/idUSTRE53S3NK20090429; Democracy Now, *War and Peace Report*, daily TV and radio news program, hosted by Amy Goodman and Juan Gonzalez, Headlines for May 29, 2009, http://www.democracynow.org/2009/5/29/headlines; Benjamin M. Friedman, "The Failure of the Economy & the Economists," *New York Review of Books*, vol. 56, no. 9, May 28, 2009, p. 42; and Bob Willis, "U.S. Economy: GDP Shrinks in Worst Slump in 50 Years (Bloomberg's Update 3)," April 29, 2009 (accessed May 27, 2009), http://www.bloomberg.com/apps/news?pid=20601068&sid=a6WLEZ20yerY; and De-

mocracy Now, *War and Peace Report*, daily TV and radio news program, hosted by Amy Goodman and Juan Gonzalez, Headlines for June 1, 2009, http://www .democracynow.org/2009/6/1/headlines.

4. Daniel Bases, "UPDATE 1—UN Revises Global Economic Growth Lower for 2009," May 27, 2009, 12:12 P.M. EDT (accessed May 28, 2009), http://www.reuters. com/article/marketsNews/idUSN2713305020090527; and Daniel Bases, "UN Revises Global Economic Growth Lower for 2009," May 27, 2009. 11:06 A.M. EDT (accessed May 28, 2009), http://www.reuters.com/article/bondsNews/ idUSN2751739520090527.

5. "Economic Downturn Leaves 26 Million Unemployed in China," *Telegraph* (United Kingdom), February 2, 2009 (accessed May 27, 2009), http://www.telegraph. co.uk/news/worldnews/asia/china/4438965/Economic-downturn-leaves-26 -million-unemployed-in-China.html; and "China's Unemployed Migrant Workers Could Top 20 Million," ABC News, March 25, 2009 (accessed May 27, 2009), http://www.abc.net.au/news/stories/2009/03/25/2526402.htm.

6. "U.S. Economy to Contract 2pc This Year, Says Fed," *Telegraph* (United Kingdom), May 21, 2009 (accessed May 27, 2009), http://www.telegraph.co.uk/finance/ financetopics/recession/5359481/US-economy-to-contract-2pc-this-year-says-Fed. html.

7. "The Crisis and How to Deal with It," *New York Review of Books*, June 11, 2009.

8. Democracy Now, *War and Peace Report*, daily TV and radio news program, hosted by Amy Goodman and Juan Gonzalez, Headlines for May 28, 2009, http://www. democracynow.org/2009/5/28/headlines.

9. Democracy Now, *War and Peace Report*, Headlines for June 1, 2009.

10. "The Crisis and How to Deal with It," *New York Review of Books*, June 11, 2009, pp. 73–76.

11. "A Silent War," Jubilee USA Network (accessed July 26, 2007), http://www. jubileeusa.org/resources/debt-resources/beginners-guide-to-debt/a-silent-war. html.

CHAPTER 2

1. Thom Hartmann, *Threshold: The Crisis of Western Culture* (New York: Viking, 2009), advance uncorrected proof, p. 145.

2. Democracy Now, *War and Peace Report*, daily TV and radio news program, hosted by Amy Goodman and Juan Gonzalez, "Michael Parenti: Economic Crisis the

Inevitable Result of 'Capitalism's Self-Inflicted Apocalypse,'" March 12, 2009, http://www.democracynow.org/2009/3/12/parenti.

3. Hartmann, *Threshold*, p. 52.

4. Democracy Now, *War and Peace Report*, daily TV and radio news program, hosted by Amy Goodman and Juan Gonzalez, Headlines for March 16, 2009, http://www.democracynow.org/2009/3/16/headlines.

5. Democracy Now, *War and Peace Report*, daily TV and radio news program, hosted by Amy Goodman and Juan Gonzalez, Headlines for March 4, 2009, http://www.democracynow.org/2009/3/4/headlines.

6. Ibid.

7. Louise Story, "Lawmakers Question Bankers on Bailout," *New York Times*, February 11, 2009, http://www.nytimes.com/2009/02/12/business/12bank.html?scp=4&sq=eight%20bankers&st=cse.

8. "Texas Firm Accused of $8 Billion Fraud," *New York Times*, February 17, 2009, http://www.nytimes.com/2009/02/18/business/18stanford.html?scp=5&sq=stanford%20group&st=cse.

9. John Schwartz, "Contrite Over Misstep, Auto Chiefs Take to the Road," *New York Times*, December 2, 2008, http://www.nytimes.com/2008/12/03/business/03jets.html.

10. Democracy Now, *War and Peace Report*, daily TV and radio news program, hosted by Amy Goodman and Juan Gonzalez, Headlines for April 14, 2009, http://www.democracynow.org/2009/4/14/headlines.

11. Ibid.

12. Ibid.

13. Democracy Now, *War and Peace Report*, Headlines for April 15, 2009, http://www.democracynow.org/2009/4/15/headlines.

14. Arianna Huffington, "Why Are Bankers Still Being Treated As Royalty?" Huffington Post, April 30, 2009, http://www.huffingtonpost.com/arianna-huffington/why-are-bankers-still-bei_b_194242.html.

15. Democracy Now, *War and Peace Report*, daily TV and radio news program, hosted by Amy Goodman and Juan Gonzalez, Headlines for May 6, 2009, http://www.democracynow.org/2009/5/6/headlines.

CHAPTER 4

1. For more about Claudine and her disappearance, see John Perkins, *Confessions of an Economic Hit Man* (New York: Penguin Group/Plume, 2004), pp. xiii–xiv; 16–21; 60–62.

2. For more about Farhad and the escape from Iran , see Perkins, *Confessions*, pp. 6; 137–39.

3. Center for Responsive Politics, OpenSecrets.org, "Stats at a Glance," http://www.opensecrets.org.

4. http://thehill.com/business—lobby/companies-hire-washington-lobbyists -before-bad-news-breaks-2006–01–31.html; and Democracy Now, *War and Peace Report*, daily TV and radio news program, hosted by Amy Goodman and Juan Gonzalez, " 'Sold Out': New Report Follows Lobbying Money Trail Behind Deregulation That Helped Cause Financial Crisis," March 4, 2009, http://www.democracynow.org/2009/3/4/sold_out_new_report_follows_lobbying.

5. Wall Street Watch, "$5 Billion in Political Contributions Bought Wall Street Freedom from Regulation, Restraint, Report Finds," March 4, 2009, http://www.wallstreetwatch.org/soldoutreport.htm.

6. Media Reform Information Center, "Number of Corporations That Control a Majority of U.S. Media," (chart), http://www.corporations.org/media/.

7. Both the power plant and NBC stories are from firsthand accounts by several people who were personally involved and, for obvious reasons, wish to remain anonymous.

8. For more information on Jim Keady and Leslie Kretzu, see John Perkins, *The Secret History of the American Empire: The Truth About Economic Hit Men, Jackals, and How to Change the World* (New York: Penguin Group/Plume, 2007), pp. 39–43; 59–61. See also the website for the Educating for Justice (EFJ) nonprofit organization (headquartered in Asbury Park, N.J.): http://www.educatingforjustice.org.

CHAPTER 5

1. Michael Hennigan, Analysis/Comment: "Executive Pay and Inequality in the Winner-take-all Society," Finfacts.com, Ireland's Business & Finance Portal, August 7, 2005 (accessed June 10, 2009), http://www.finfacts.com/irelandbusinessnews/publish/printer_10002825.shtml.

2. Ralph Waldo Emerson, *Wealth* essay, in *The Conduct of Life*, 1860, revised 1876, http://www.emersoncentral.com/wealth.htm.

CHAPTER 6

1. BBC News, "Ecuador Defaults on Foreign Debt," December 12, 2008 (accessed June 24, 2009), http://news.bbc.co.uk/2/hi/business/7780984.stm.

2. Anthony Faiola, "Calling Foreign Debt 'Immoral,' Leader Allows Ecuador to Default," *Washington Post,* December 13, 2008 (accessed June 24, 2009), http://www.washingtonpost.com/wp-dyn/content/article/2008/12/12/AR2008121204105.html.

3. To see an award-winning documentary about the Ecuador situation and lawsuit, go to the website http://www.crudethemovie.com.

4. Neil Watkins and Sarah Anderson, "Ecuador's Debt Default: Exposing a Gap in the Global Financial Architecture," *Foreign Policy In Focus,* December 15, 2008 (accessed June 25, 2009), http://www.fpif.org/fpiftxt/5744.

5. Lucy Adams, "Plight of Women Sold into Slavery Revealed," *Herald* (Glasgow, Scotland), April 19, 2008 (accessed May 1, 2009), http://www.theherald.co.uk/news/news/display.var.2428222.0.plight_of_women_sold_into_slavery_revealed.php.

6. Joel Brinkley, "Vast Trade in Forced Labor Portrayed in C.I.A. Report," *New York Times,* April 2, 2000 (accessed May 1, 2009), http://www.nytimes.com/2000/04/02/us/vast-trade-in-forced-labor-portrayed-in-cia-report.html?sec=&spon=&&.

7. Stacey Hirsh, "Reagan Presidency Pivotal for Unions," *Baltimore Sun,* June 8, 2004 (accessed June 26, 2009), http://www.baltimoresun.com/business/bal-bz.unions08jun08,0,1761456.story?coll=bal-business-headlines.

8. Julie Hirschfeld Davis, Associated Press writer, "The Influence Game: Payday Lenders Thwart Limits," ABC News, April 2, 2009, http://abcnews.go.com/International/wireStory?id=7242991.

9. Democracy Now, *War and Peace Report,* daily TV and radio news program, hosted by Amy Goodman and Juan Gonzalez, "Ecuadorian President: World Should Consider Abolishing IMF," Headlines for June 26, 2009, http://www.democracynow.org/2009/6/26/headlines.

CHAPTER 7

1. "The Rise and Fall of Dennis Kozlowski: How Did He Become So Unhinged by Greed? A Revealing Look at the Man Behind the Tyco Scandal," *BusinessWeek,* December 23, 2002 (accessed July 10, 2009), http://www.businessweek.com/magazine/content/02_51/b3813001.htm.

2. "Inside Stephen Schwarzman's Birthday Bash," *New York Times*, February 14, 2007 (accessed July 11, 2009), http://dealbook.blogs.nytimes.com/2007/02/14/inside-stephen-schwarzmans-birthday-bash/.

3. Nelson D. Schwartz, "Wall Street's Man of the Moment," *Fortune*, CNNMoney.com, February 21, 2007 (accessed July 11, 2009), http://money.cnn.com/magazines/fortune/fortune_archive/2007/03/05/8401261/index.htm.

4. www.cbsnews.com/stories/2006/06/28/national/main1758528.shtml.

5. CleanUpGE.org, "Toxics on the Hudson: The Story of GE, PCBs and the Hudson River," undated (accessed July 18, 2009), http://www.cleanupge.org/pcbarticle.pdf.

6. Ibid.

7. "The World's Billionaires," edited by Luisa Kroll, Matthew Miller, and Tatiana Serafin, *Forbes*, March 11, 2009 (accessed July 18, 2009), http://www.forbes.com/2009/03/11/worlds-richest-people-billionaires-2009-billionaires_land.html; and Duncan Greenberg and Tatiana Serafin, "Billionaires List: Up in Smoke," *Forbes*, March 30, 2009 (accessed July 18, 2009), http://www.forbes.com/forbes/2009/0330/076-up-in-smoke.html.

8. Warren Vieth, "Most U.S. Firms Paid No Income Taxes in '90s: More Than Half Avoided Levies During Boom Years," *Los Angeles Times*, April 11, 2004, http://www.boston.com/business/globe/articles/2004/04/11/most_us_firms_paid_no_income_taxes_in_90s/.

9. David Goldman, "Most Firms Pay No Income Taxes—Congress," CNNMoney.com, August 12, 2008 (accessed July 19, 2009), http://money.cnn.com/2008/08/12/news/economy/corporate_taxes.

10. "Who Is Poor?" Institute for Research on Poverty (IRP), posted December 6, 2004 (accessed July 13, 2009), http://www.irp.wisc.edu/faqs/faq3.htm. See also Anuradha Mittal, "Hunger in America," CommonDreams.org, December 10, 2004 (accessed July 18, 2009), http://www.commondreams.org/views04/1210–22.htm.

11. U.S. Census figures reported by the National Coalition on Health Care (NCHC), "Health Insurance Coverage," Washington, D.C., posted 2009 (accessed July 18, 2009), http://www.nchc.org/facts/coverage.shtml.

12. G. William Domhoff, "Wealth, Income, and Power," Who Rules America website, September 2005, updated May 2009 (accessed July 13, 2009), http://sociology.ucsc.edu/whorulesamerica/power/wealth.html.

CHAPTER 8

1. For details about IPS, its competitors, and its success, see John Perkins, *The Stress-Free Habit: Powerful Techniques for Health and Longevity from the Andes, Yucatan, and Far East* (Rochester, Vt.: Healing Arts Press, 1989); and John Perkins, *Shapeshifting: Shamanic Techniques for Global and Personal Transformation* (Rochester, Vt.: Destiny Books, 1997).

2. 132 *Congressional Record*. S8272–73 (daily edition June 24, 1986. Colloquy of Senators Baucus and Packwood).

3. Harvey Wasserman, "California's Deregulation Disaster," *The Nation*, February 12, 2001, http://www.thenation.com/doc/20010212/wasserman.

4. FERC 3–26–03 Docket No. PA02–2-000, *Staff Report Price Manipulation in Western Markets*"; and http://www.sfgate.com/cgi-bin/article.cgi?f=/c/a/2000/12/08/MN148567.DTL.

CHAPTER 9

1. Daniel Engber, "Why Do Airlines Go Bankrupt: Delta Can't Keep up with JetBlue," Slate Magazine, September 15, 2005, http://www.slate.com/id/2126383/.

2. Thom Hartmann, *Threshold: The Crisis of Western Culture* (New York: Viking, 2009), advance uncorrected proof, pp. 39; 41.

CHAPTER 10

1. "Amazon Crude: Scott Pelley Reports on a Multi-Billion-Dollar Lawsuit over Oil Drilling Pollution" *60 Minutes*, CBS, May 3, 2009, http://www.cbsnews.com/stories/2009/05/01/60minutes/main4983549.shtml.

2. "Toward a More Sustainable Way of Business," http://www.interfaceglobal.com/Sustainability.aspx.

CHAPTER 11

1. "Suspended Nicaraguan Priest Elected President of U.N. General Assembly," Catholic News Agency, June 6, 2008 (accessed June 30, 2009), http://www.catholicnewsagency.com/new.php?n=12862.

2. Structural Adjustment Participatory Review International Network (SAPRIN), Washington, D.C., letter to James Wolfensohn, President, World Bank, April 16, 2004 (accessed June 1, 2009), http://www.developmentgap.org/worldbank_imf/

saprin_letter_to_world_bank_president_16april2004.pdf. See also on the organization's website "The Development GAP's Mission and Operating Principles":
http://www.developmentgap.org/mission%26principles/mission_principles.
html.

CHAPTER 12

1. "The Crisis and How to Deal with It," *New York Review of Books*, June 11, 2009,
   p. 76.

2. Barbara Hagenbaugh, "U.S. Manufacturing Jobs Fading Away Fast," *USA TODAY*,
   December 12, 2002, http://www.usatoday.com/money/economy/2002–12–12
   -manufacture_x.htm.

3. Andrew Gumbel, "How the War Machine Is Driving the U.S. Economy," *Independent* (United Kingdom), January 6, 2004, http://www.commondreams.org/
   views04/0106–12.htm.

4. NPR, *Weekend Edition Sunday*, hosted by Linda Wertheimer, April 5, 2009, http://
   www.npr.org.

5. "2008 Global Arms Spending Hits Record High," *China Daily*, June 9, 2009, from
   Reuters and Associated Press, p. 11. See also Democracy Now, *War and Peace Report*, daily TV and radio news program, hosted by Amy Goodman and Juan Gonzalez, "Report: Global Military Spending Rose to $1.46 Trillion in 2008," Headlines
   for June 8, 2009, http://www.democracynow.org/2009/6/8/headlines.

6. See the following websites: http://www.gpoaccess.gov/usbudget/fy09/pdf/
   budget/defense.pdf; http://www.slate.com/id/2183592/pagenum/all/; http://
   www.truthandpolitics.org/military-relative-size.php; http://www.defenselink.
   mil/comptroller/defbudget/fy2008/fy2008_weabook.pdf; and http://www.
   globalissues.org/article/75/world-military-spending.

7. See the following websites: http://www.warresisters.org/pages/piechart.htm;
   http://www.globalissues.org/article/75/world-military-spending; and http://
   www.slate.com/id/2183592/pagenum/all/.

8. See the websites listed in note 6 above.

9. See the websites listed in note 7 above.

10. See also Democracy Now, *War and Peace Report*, daily TV and radio news program,
    hosted by Amy Goodman and Juan Gonzalez, Headlines for May 11, 2009, http://
    www.democracynow.org/2009/5/11/headlines.

CONCLUSION

1. Mark Weisbrot, "Who's in Charge of U.S. Foreign Policy? The Coup in Honduras Has Exposed Divisions between Barack Obama and His Secretary of State, Hillary Clinton," *Guardian* (United Kingdom), July 16, 2009 (accessed July 23, 2009), http://www.guardian.co.uk/commentisfree/cifamerica/2009/jul/16/honduras-coup-obama-clinton.

2. Democracy Now, *War and Peace Report*, daily TV and radio news program, hosted by Amy Goodman and Juan Gonzalez, "From Arbenz to Zelaya: Chiquita in Latin America," July 21, 2009 (accessed July 23, 2009), http://www.democracynow.org/2009/7/21/from_arbenz_to_zelaya_chiquita_in.

3. "Chiquita Admits to Paying Colombia Terrorists: Banana Company Agrees to $25 Million Fine for Paying AUC for Protection," Associated Press, MSNBC, March 15, 2007 (accessed July 24, 2009), http://www.msnbc.msn.com/id/17615143/.

4. For more information, see Alex Constantine's Blacklist, "AG Eric Holder & Chiquita, Covington, Negroponte, Bolton, Colombian Death Squads," July 20, 2009 (accessed July 23, 2009), http://aconstantineblacklist.blogspot.com/2009/07/eric-holder-and-chiquita-covington.html.

5. Mark Weisbrot, "The High-Powered Hidden Support for Honduras' Coup: The Country's Rightful President Was Ousted by a Military Leadership That Takes Many of Its Cues from Washington Insiders," *Los Angeles Times*, July 23, 2009, http://www.latimes.com/news/opinion/commentary/la-oe-weisbrot23-2009jul23,0,7566740.story.

Index

About the Author

John Perkins had the official title of Chief Economist at a major international consulting firm during the 1970s. He advised the World Bank, United Nations, International Monetary Fund (IMF), U.S. Treasury Department, Fortune 500 corporations, and countries in Africa, Asia, Latin America, and the Middle East. In his role as economic hit man, he worked directly with heads of state and CEOs of major companies to promote and develop the types of projects described in *Hoodwinked* and *Confessions of an Economic Hit Man,* a book that spent more than sixty-five weeks on the *New York Times* bestseller list. He has been published in over thirty languages and is required reading at universities and business schools in the United States and many other countries.

During the 1980s he was CEO of an alternative energy company that was a pioneer in developing environmentally beneficial power plants. He devoted much of his time in the 1990s and 2000s not only to writing and lecturing, but also to establishing and supporting Dream Change, The Pachamama Alliance, and other nonprofit organizations that are committed to creating a sustainable, just, and peaceful world.

In addition to his books on economics and geopolitics—*Hoodwinked, Confessions of an Economic Hit Man,* and *The Secret History of the American Empire*—he has also written the following books about indigenous cultures and personal and global transformation: *Shapeshifting, The World Is as You Dream It, Psychonavigation, Spirit of the Shuar,* and *The Stress-Free Habit.*

For more information or to contact John Perkins, please visit: www.johnperkins.org and www.dreamchange.org.